Peter's

An adventure game based on
J. M. Barrie's
Peter Pan and Wendy

Illustrated by Peter Stevenson

HODDER AND STOUGHTON
LONDON SYDNEY AUCKLAND TORONTO

Do you know that this book is part of J. M. Barrie's Peter Pan gift? This means that Sir James Barrie's royalty on this book goes to help sick children at the Great Ormond Street Hospital for Sick Children in London, to whom Sir James Barrie bequeathed the copyright of Peter Pan.

British Library Cataloguing in Publication Data

Peter's revenge: an adventure game based on J. M. Barrie's Peter Pan
  and Wendy.—(Adventure games book).
  1. Adventure games—Juvenile literature
  I. Barrie, J. M. Peter Pan and Wendy
  II. Stevenson, Peter, 1953–   III. Series
  793'.9   GV1203

ISBN 0-340-41316-6

Text copyright © Stephen Thraves 1987
Illustrations copyright © Hodder and Stoughton Ltd 1987

First published 1987

All rights reserved. No part of this publication may be reproduced or transmitted in any form or by any means, electronically or mechanically, including photocopying, recording, or any information storage and retrieval system, without either the prior permission in writing from the publisher or a licence, permitting restricted copying, issued by the Copyright Licensing Agency, 33–34 Alfred Place, London WC1E 7DP.

Published by Hodder and Stoughton Children's Books,
a division of Hodder and Stoughton Ltd,
Mill Road, Dunton Green, Sevenoaks, Kent TN13 2YJ

Photoset by Rowland Phototypesetting Ltd,
Bury St Edmunds, Suffolk

Printed in Great Britain by Hazell, Watson & Viney Ltd,
Member of the BPCC Group,
Aylesbury, Bucks

The story of Peter Pan and his magical adventures has been delighting young readers for years. Peter's first visit to the children through their bedroom window, his whisking them off to Neverland, his skirmishes with the dreaded Captain Hook . . . these are episodes that many of you must know off by heart.

But have you ever secretly wished that you could go one step further? That you could actually *take part* in these adventures? Well, now you can! This Peter Pan Adventure Game Book invites you to fly along with the children, directing them in their escapades. Using various special cards to assist you, you have to guide them to their journey's end.

You will not necessarily achieve this on your first attempt. It may well take several goes. Keep trying, though, and you will eventually be successful.

Even when you have been successful, the game can still be played again. For there are many different routes to the game – each route involving different stories and activities.

So, the game can be played over and over . . . as many times as you like!

HOW TO PLAY

The object of the game is to guide Peter and the children through a series of escapades. You do this by starting at PARAGRAPH ONE and then following the instructions to other paragraphs.

Many of the paragraphs will involve you in some sort of activity. It might be trying to work out where you are in Neverland or trying to interpret what a particular Neverlander is saying. You do not have to be successful at *every one* of the activities to guide the children to their journey's end . . . but the more you can do, the more chance you'll have. *To help you* in these activities, there are several useful items Peter and the children can carry for you on the journey. These are a map of Neverland, a telescope, a Neverland dictionary and a book of magic spells. You can start with only *one* of these ITEMS but you will often pick up others as the journey progresses.

The ITEM chosen for them to start with (and any items they gain later) is to be kept, during the game, in the slit of the CHARACTER CARD – the one depicting Peter and the children. This will tell you exactly which ITEMS you, and they, have for assistance at any one time (so, as soon as one of these ITEMS has helped in a particular activity, always remember to return it to the CHARACTER CARD). Any ITEMS not contained in the slit of the CHARACTER CARD are not to be used or consulted – and should therefore be kept out of play.

The journey to Neverland can only be made by flying. Peter Pan and Tinker Bell were born with the ability to fly but for their three friends (rather more normal children!) this doesn't come naturally. In fact, because Wendy, John and Michael can only fly with the help of an occasional sprinkling of fairy dust, you must take three FAIRY DUST CARDS on the journey. These should be kept in the slit of the TOP-HAT CARD. Every time the children need another sprinkling of fairy dust (or lose one of the pouches), you must remove one of the FAIRY DUST CARDS from the TOP-HAT CARD. When there are no FAIRY DUST CARDS left in the TOP-HAT CARD, it means that the children only just have enough flying power to return home – and you must immediately end their adventure. Of course you can always start another game – with a new supply of cards – from the beginning!

THE CHARACTERS ON YOUR DICE

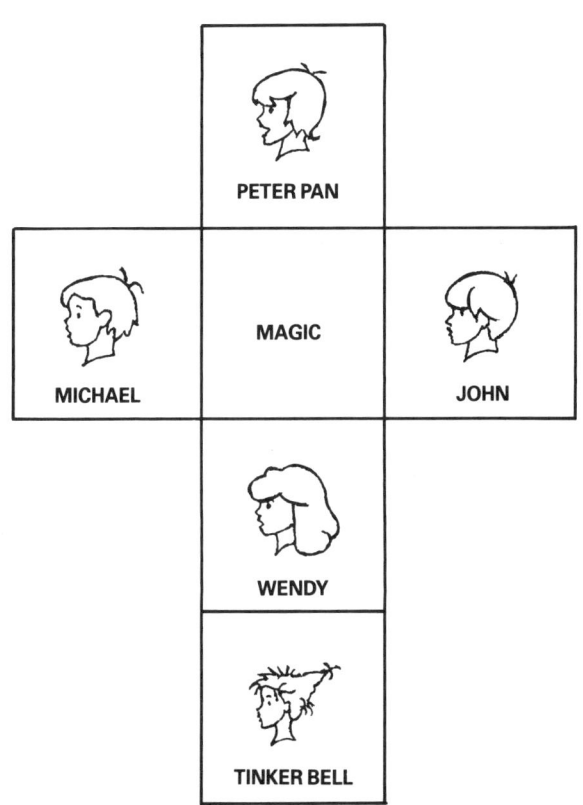

READY TO START!

It is a chill winter night. The stars are twinkling rather mischievously in the clear sky. At No. 14, three children – Wendy, John and Michael – sleep soundly in their beds. Their parents, Mr and Mrs Darling, are dining out for the evening . . . but there's no need for worry, there are night lights in the children's bedroom and the window is securely locked.

But suddenly the window blows open and a strange-looking boy flies in. He is clad in leaves and has an elfin face. It is Peter Pan! There is someone else with him, a beautiful fairy that darts about in trails of light. She is his jealous admirer, Tinker Bell.

Peter has made this visit for a reason. His home is a magical island many many miles and dreams away – called Neverland. It is a place where all *lost boys* go: boys who were neglected as babies and fell out of their prams. On the whole, these lost boys have a very exciting time because Neverland is also home to many strange and wonderful creatures . . . and to redskins and pirates! Hardly a day goes by without some enthralling battle or other.

But there is just one thing they envy normal children for. They have no mother to tuck them in at night and tell them stories. So, they have sent Peter to find them one.

Looking in at all the windows, Peter has decided that Wendy would make the absolute perfect mother. It doesn't matter that she's not quite grown up yet. In fact, Peter has a deep dislike of grown-ups. Yes, Wendy would do perfectly!

When Wendy is woken up, she seems entirely agreeable to Peter's proposal. She finds him so delightful, how can she possibly refuse? But she insists that John and Michael come with them as well. So, all three of them prepare to fly off to Neverland . . .

To join them on this trip, first pick out the card showing Peter Pan and the children and keep it near to you. Peter has brought with him four different ITEMS that he thought might be useful on their journey. These are a *map of Neverland*, a *Neverland dictionary* (to interpret what the Neverlanders are saying), a *telescope* and a *book of magic spells* (to get them out of sticky situations!). Unfortunately, though, he is very careless and forgetful, and he leaves three of the ITEMS behind in the children's bedroom. Still, he does remember to take one – and your next task is to choose which ITEM this should be. Which do you think would be the most useful on the journey? Insert the ITEM you choose into the *slit* of the CHARACTER CARD and keep the remaining three ITEMS out of play until such time as you are told to pick them up.

Now to sort out about the fairy dust. You'll remember that the three Darling children are only able to fly if they are sprinkled with this. Peter gives them all a generous sprinkle before they set off but it is such a long journey to Neverland that they'll need further sprinkles on the way. Peter therefore hands the children three pouches of fairy dust as reserve, suggesting John put them in his top-hat for safe-keeping. So, also place the TOP-HAT CARD near you and insert the three FAIRY DUST CARDS in the slit.

Don't forget to remove a FAIRY DUST CARD every time you are instructed during the game. And, remember, when there are no FAIRY DUST CARDS left in the TOP-HAT CARD, you must immediately stop that particular game and start the adventure all over again from the beginning (try starting with a different ITEM this time to see if it gives you any more luck).

Happy Adventuring!

1

'Ooh, isn't flying wonderful!' said the three Darling children together as they all floated out of the window and followed Peter and Tinker Bell high above the rooftops. They spread out their arms as wide as they would go, giving them a little flap every now and then. It was just as they imagined flying should be! 'Which way is Neverland?' John asked excitedly, and Peter pointed in the direction of a little star that blinked at them in the distance. Before they started off, though, Wendy insisted that they arrange themselves in some sort of order. Well brought up children don't wander all over the place when they go for a walk and nor should they when they fly! 'Come on now, everyone in a nice neat line,' she ordered bossily. 'We'll only have one person at the front, thank you very much. Now, who's it going to be?'

To decide who is going to fly at the front, throw the special DICE – then turn to the appropriate number. If you throw 'Magic', you must turn to that number instead.

PETER thrown	go to 58
TINKER BELL thrown	go to 31
WENDY thrown	go to 13
JOHN thrown	go to 205
MICHAEL thrown	go to 142
MAGIC thrown	go to 101

2

Having found the castle on the map, Peter suggested that they all enter it. 'Oh, we couldn't possibly,' Wendy said. 'Look at all those horrible bats flying around!' It was the bats that seemed to fascinate Peter, though! 'We could fly round the turrets chasing them,' he suggested excitedly, 'or we could pretend to be bats ourselves, hissing and flapping!' Wendy gave a firm no, though, saying that they would probably have enough adventures as it was – without going to look for them! ***Go to 123.***

3

Since Peter didn't have a telescope, he would just have to leave it to his fancy as to whether that was Captain Hook's ship or not. His fancy decided that it was! 'Is Captain Hook a friend of yours, then?' Michael asked him with interest. Peter's eyes lit up with passion. 'No!' he replied keenly, practising a few deadly thrusts with his sword. 'He's my arch-enemy!' ***Go to 253.***

4

'Oh, is that one, over there?' Wendy cried a few minutes later as she suddenly spotted what looked like an ice-cream tree. There were cornets of ice-cream growing from every branch and so it certainly seemed as if it might be! 'Yes, that's one,' Peter confirmed and he hurriedly led the way towards it. They all flew up into the branches to pluck their favourite flavour but Peter couldn't find his. 'There's no chocolate!' he exclaimed. Since he looked about to cry, Wendy quickly suggested using his magic spell book to magic some!

Use your MAGIC SPELL BOOK to find the right magic word for this by placing exactly over the shape below – then follow the appropriate instruction. If you don't have one, you'll have to guess which instruction to follow.

If you think it's SHIMMER	go to 81
If you think it's TWINKLE	go to 198
If you think it's SPARKLE	go to 224

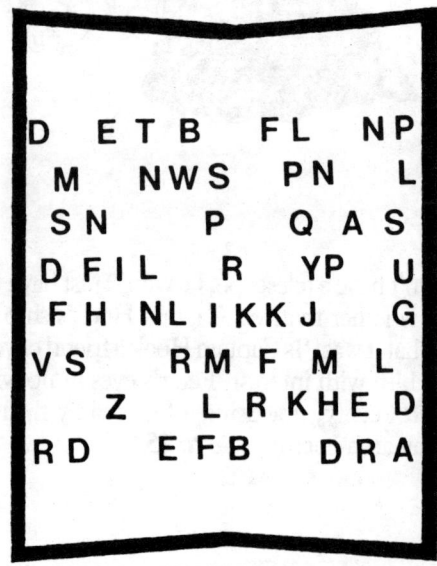

5

It's not fair, thought John, huddled in his crow's-nest, as the pirates' ship sailed on and on. Peter won't mind steering the ship because he likes being in charge of things. Wendy won't mind swabbing the decks because she can't bear places being dirty anyway. And Michael and Tinker Bell won't mind working in the kitchens because they can pinch a few biscuits now and then! But it was then that John found a telescope in the crow's-nest – one of the finest telescopes he had seen. So perhaps *his* job had its perks as well!

If you don't already have it there, put the TELESCOPE CARD into your CHARACTER CARD. Now go to 77.

6

Using Peter's dictionary to translate what the redskin chief was saying, the children gave an enormous sigh of relief. He was merely asking them to smoke a peace-pipe with him. John and Michael were delighted at the idea – they had never smoked a peace-pipe before – but Wendy was a little cautious. She told her brothers that it might taste as bad as the medicine they sometimes had to take . . . maybe even worse. But she didn't wish to offend the chief and so she agreed that they should all have just a little puff. As it turned out, it didn't taste too bad and the chief was so honoured by their action that he gave them a magic spell book as a gift.

If you don't already have it there, put the MAGIC SPELL BOOK CARD into your CHARACTER CARD. Now go to 125.

7

A tiny little tinkle of bells showed that *Tinker Bell* had woken first. Life is very short for a fairy and so she didn't want to waste too much of it sleeping! Of course, if she had been a considerate fairy she would have had breakfast prepared for when the others awoke. Sadly, though, she wasn't very considerate and so the others opened their eyes to an empty table. But what was a table doing there in the cave, anyway? And how about that large cauldron in the corner? Suddenly, Peter realised. 'It's a witches' cavern,' he explained. 'They must have been out for the night, flying around on their broomsticks.' Wendy thought it would be a good idea to look up the cavern on their map to find out exactly where they were.

Use your MAP to find which square the witches' cavern is in – then follow the appropriate instruction. If you don't have one, you'll have to guess which instruction to follow.

If you think B1	go to 235
If you think C1	go to 20
If you think B2	go to 218

8

The children soon encountered the polar bear they had come there to see. It was plunging from an ice-drift into the freezing blue-green water. Peter couldn't resist the opportunity to prove that he was just as good a diver himself, by flying a few metres up into the air and then piercing the water's surface. This goaded John and Michael into doing the same, although they weren't immune to the icy cold as was Peter. In fact, it was such a shock to them that they found they had lost all their flying power and had to have another sprinkle of fairy dust to restore it!

Remove one of the FAIRY DUST CARDS from your TOP-HAT CARD. Now go to 181.

9

'*MOLAR!*' exclaimed Peter just as the crocodile was about to snap at their toes – and suddenly all its teeth dropped out! The crocodile felt rather pathetic without its nice razor-sharp teeth and so immediately withdrew, crawling sheepishly back into the water. Wendy began to feel a little sorry for it but Peter told her that its teeth would soon grow back. The children were just preparing to take to the air again when John found a pirate's telescope at the edge of the creek. 'It probably belonged to that fiend, Captain Hook!' said Peter as he tucked it under his belt.

If you don't already have it there, put the TELESCOPE CARD into your CHARACTER CARD. Now go to 118.

10

John entered the tree first, squeezing in through a large squirrel-hole. As soon as John had slid down, Michael followed . . . then Wendy, then Peter, then Tinker Bell. 'Hello, lost boys!' Peter called out when they had all reached the underground home. 'I've brought a mother for you!' But the lost boys were nowhere to be found – not even hiding under the beds! 'Something must have happened to them!' Peter said with growing concern. His fears seemed to be confirmed when he found a note pinned to the wall. It was written in Neverlander, though, so they could only decipher what it said with the help of a dictionary.

Use your NEVERLAND DICTIONARY to find out what the note said by translating the instruction below. If you don't have one, go to 111 instead.

DIDDLY PUTT
TRIX ISH

11

The fight between Peter and Hook seemed to go on and on forever, their swords rattled and clashed until the sparks flew. At first it looked as if Peter had the upper hand but then Hook began to take control and Wendy and Tinker Bell hid their eyes. Peter thrust his sword at Hook, missing his enemy's head by a hair's-breadth, then Hook's sword jabbed only centimetres from Peter's heart. Finally, though, Peter began to wear his enemy down, forcing him on to the bulwarks. He was about to make one last lunge at Hook when he saw the gleaming open jaws of a crocodile in the water beneath – the very crocodile to whom he had once tossed Hook's severed right hand! A thought occurred to Peter, why not feed it the rest of him? So, he gently nudged his arch-enemy over the side of the ship . . . and that was the end of Captain Hook! ***Go to 131.***

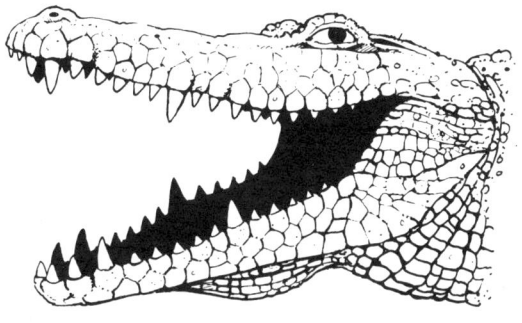

12

Peter walked over to one of the rum barrels, lifting it above his head and pulling out the cork. 'I can down one of these in three gulps,' he said, as the dark liquid poured into his throat. 'That's better than any pirate!' he added. John and Michael thought they would like to try some of the rum too and uncorked one of the other barrels. A few drops, though, and they were as dizzy as anything – and when they tried to fly they found that they could barely leave the ground! 'We'd best have another sprinkle of fairy dust!' said a decidedly queasy-feeling John.

Remove one of the FAIRY DUST CARDS from your TOP-HAT CARD. Now go to 176.

13

There was so much arguing about who was to fly at the front that Wendy decided she had better take the lead herself! Peter was, to say the least, a little bewildered as he found himself obediently following behind her. *He* had always been used to being the leader. So was this what mothers were like! Wendy had led them all a good few miles when a disaster happened. An unfriendly cloud decided to swallow them all up! 'Never mind,' said Peter casually as they groped around in the thick white mist, 'I'll use my magic spell book. I only have to find the right word and we'll immediately be out of it!' But then an awful thought occurred to him. Had he left the magic spell book behind in the children's bedroom?

Do you have the MAGIC SPELL BOOK CARD in the slit of your CHARACTER CARD? If so, use it to find the right spell

word by placing exactly over the shape below – then follow the appropriate instruction. *(Remember to return the MAGIC SPELL BOOK to the CHARACTER CARD afterwards.)* If you don't have one, you'll have to guess which instruction to follow.

If you think it's MUSHROOM	go to 163
If you think it's TOADSTOOL	go to 185
If you think it's FOXGLOVE	go to 270

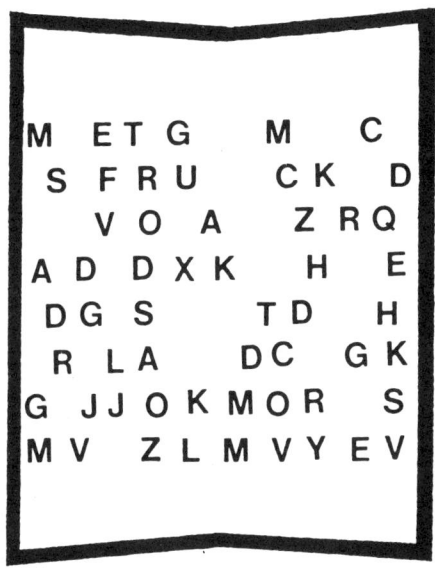

14

Peter's map showed them that the pink cliffs were in the extreme south-west corner of the island. 'Right, let's begin our adventure,' Peter said excitedly, drawing his sword. Unfortunately, adventures didn't always happen exactly when you wanted them and that seemed to be the case now. There wasn't an adventure anywhere around! 'Never mind, Peter, I'm sure we'll come across one soon,' Wendy told him kindly. And to make him feel a little better she handed him a magic spell book she had just found in the grass.

If you don't already have it there, put the MAGIC SPELL BOOK CARD in the slit of your CHARACTER CARD. Now go to 197.

15

Hardly had Peter uttered the word *RAINBOW* than one of the lost boys appeared! The boy rubbed his eyes as if he wasn't sure what had happened to him. 'Oh, isn't he a dear!' Wendy exclaimed, quite taken by his little bear-skin clothes and his soulful face. 'What's your name, boy?' Before the boy could answer, however, the magic spell had worn off and he was suddenly whisked away again. But it had all been enough to persuade Wendy to put up with an adventure or two after all! ***Go to 208.***

16

Michael reached the redskin camp first. Never having seen a real live Indian before, he had flown as fast as he possibly could! 'Don't go too near them, Michael, in case they're on the warpath,' Wendy cautioned him when she also arrived . . . but it was too late because Michael had strolled right into their midst! There was nothing to fear, though, because, far from being in a war mood, they seemed quite down and dejected. When Peter asked them what was wrong, the chief drew pictures for him in the ground with an arrow. 'He says that his daughter, Tiger Lily, has been abducted by Captain Hook's pirates,' he informed the others gravely. 'She has been taken to Wailing Lake and left on a rock to drown. We must rescue her!'

Use your MAP to find which square Wailing Lake is in – then follow the appropriate instruction. If you don't have one, you'll have to guess which instruction to follow.

If you think B2	go to 233
If you think B3	go to 214
If you think C2	go to 50

17

'*TATTOO!*' Peter cried when he had found the right word in his magic spell book – and the children suddenly found themselves on the deck of a ship. They were just laughing at how surprised the pirates on the beach must have been, however, when other pirates appeared all around them! 'We must have landed on the *Jolly Roger* – the pirates' ship!' Peter said with alarm. This was indeed so, and Captain Hook and the pirates from the beach soon joined them, having rowed out to the ship in a little boat. 'Out of the frying pan, into the fire . . .' Wendy remarked softly. ***Go to 158.***

18

Peter and the children hadn't journeyed much further through Neverland when night began to fall. Colours greyed and then greys darkened. 'It looks as if the lost boys will have to go one more night without me,' Wendy remarked as they quickly searched for somewhere to sleep. She only hoped there wasn't too much playing-up after lights out! Peter managed to find a cave just before night fell altogether and so they all crawled inside, making mossy beds for themselves. It had been a long day, full of adventures, and it wasn't long before they were all sound asleep.

Throw the special DICE to decide who is to be the first to wake in the morning.

PETER thrown	go to 52
TINKER BELL thrown	go to 7
WENDY thrown	go to 106
JOHN thrown	go to 190
MICHAEL thrown	go to 148
MAGIC thrown	go to 63

19

'There are the icebergs!' John shouted excitedly as he pointed to several huge pyramids of ice floating in the green-blue water below. No sooner had they landed on the ice than a number of Eskimoes gathered round them. 'Do you think they're friendly?' John asked anxiously, noticing the large spears in their hands. One of the Eskimoes now spoke, but it was in Neverlander so Wendy quickly asked Peter for his dictionary.

*Use your **NEVERLAND DICTIONARY** to find out what the Eskimo was saying by translating the instruction in his speech-balloon below. If you don't have one, go to 260 instead.*

20

John and Michael weren't interested in looking up the witches' cavern on their map, though. All they wanted to do was leave before the witches returned! 'They might turn us into frogs!' said John anxiously. 'They might turn us into tadpoles!' said Michael. Peter pointed out that tadpoles wouldn't be as bad as frogs because at least tadpoles hadn't grown up but the others didn't pay him much attention. They were busy preparing to leave! ***Go to 84.***

21

At last the children sighted the sea and, not long after, they sighted Hook's ship! Unfortunately, Hook also sighted *them* at the very same moment – through his telescope. He immediately went across to his cannon, aiming it at them. 'Duck your heads, everyone!' Peter cried as the cannonball came whistling in their direction. John didn't duck quickly enough, though, and the cannonball dislodged his hat! 'One of the fairy dust pouches has dropped out, Peter!' he moaned as he put the hat straight again, but his complaint went unheard. Peter was now hurriedly leading the way down to Hook's ship, whipping out his sword!

Remove a FAIRY DUST CARD from your TOP-HAT CARD. Now go to 11. (Remember: when there are no FAIRY DUST CARDS left in your TOP-HAT CARD the game is over, and you must start again from the beginning.)

22

When Peter had (rather sulkily!) found Crocodile Creek on his map, Wendy said it was about time they were off again. So John and Michael quickly gobbled up one last sausage as they prepared to leave. John was just plucking an *extra* sausage from the tree to put under his hat for the journey when he noticed a Neverland dictionary wedged between the branches. He decided to put that under his hat as well!

If you don't already have it there, put the NEVERLAND DICTIONARY CARD into your CHARACTER CARD. Now go to 118.

23

Since Peter didn't have a telescope, he suggested another idea. They could all wait up here – just treading air – while Tinker Bell went to find a nice landing-place for them. So off Tinker Bell flew, disappearing down below. 'I think I can just hear her tinkle now,' Peter said, putting his hand to his ear, after half an hour or so. 'That means she must have found somewhere,' he added excitedly. They all followed the sound of the tinkle but instead of landing on some nice soft grass as they were expecting, they bumped down on some hard rocks. If Wendy hadn't known better, she would have said Tinker Bell had done it deliberately! ***Go to 103.***

24

'I don't see why we need a dictionary anyway,' John said rather irritably when they discovered that they didn't have one. 'If the gnome could understand our question, then he must be able to speak our language. So why didn't he *answer* in our language as well!' Peter merely laughed at the logic, though, explaining that gnomes tended to be awkward creatures. John soon had even more reason for being annoyed with this gnome for, just as he was about to put his hat back on, the gnome pinched one of the pouches of fairy dust from inside. The cheeky creature ran off down the nearest rabbit-hole before John could catch him!

Remove one of the FAIRY DUST CARDS from your TOP-HAT CARD. Now go to 208.

25

Despite their fierce appearance, deep down the pirates were a cowardly lot and so they captured Wendy first. They thought she would put up less of a fight than the boys and could be used to force them to surrender. Their plan worked a treat because Peter immediately ordered John and Michael to throw down their weapons (even though they didn't have any!). 'They must be taking us to their ship,' Wendy said as the pirates roughly escorted them along the beach. She asked Peter to use his telescope to see if he could spot where the ship was moored.

*Use your **TELESCOPE** to try and spot the pirates' ship by placing exactly over the shape below – then follow the instruction. If you don't have one, go to 83 instead.*

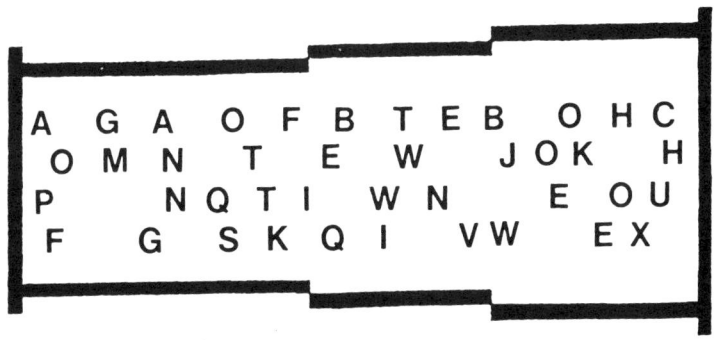

26

'*WIGWAM!*' the children all shouted together when Peter had turned to the right magic spell word in his book, and the children suddenly found themselves flying through the air. The astonished redskins grew tinier and tinier below! When the children were well out of danger, they dropped down again – landing in a haystack of pink straw. As they scrambled to their feet, Michael suddenly noticed that a telescope had appeared under his arm. Perhaps that was part of the magic spell too!

If you don't already have it there, put the TELESCOPE CARD into your CHARACTER CARD. Now go to 18.

27

The children didn't have to search long before they found a polar bear. 'Oh, isn't it delightful?' exclaimed Wendy as they watched it playing with its cubs. Peter was a little saddened at the sight, though. He'd never had a mother to care for him like that! 'Never mind, Peter,' said Wendy tenderly, reading his thoughts. 'You have me as your mother now!' ***Go to 181.***

28

Peter and the children had flown quite a few miles from Mermaid Cove when they spotted a muddy creek below them. There were a few sausage trees growing at the side of the creek and so John and

Michael suggested flying down to have a quick snack. As they were munching away at the sausages, though, a crocodile appeared in the water! 'Don't worry, it's quite safe,' Peter told the children airily. 'The only person it has a taste for is the pirate, Captain Hook. You see, I once fed it Hook's right hand after I had sliced it off . . . and the crocodile has never fancied any other human since!' Rather than being impressed by this story as Peter had hoped, Wendy merely asked him to look up Crocodile Creek on his map!

Use your MAP to find which square Crocodile Creek is in – then follow the appropriate instruction. If you don't have one, you'll have to guess which instruction to follow.

If you think B3	go to 74
If you think C3	go to 141
If you think D3	go to 22

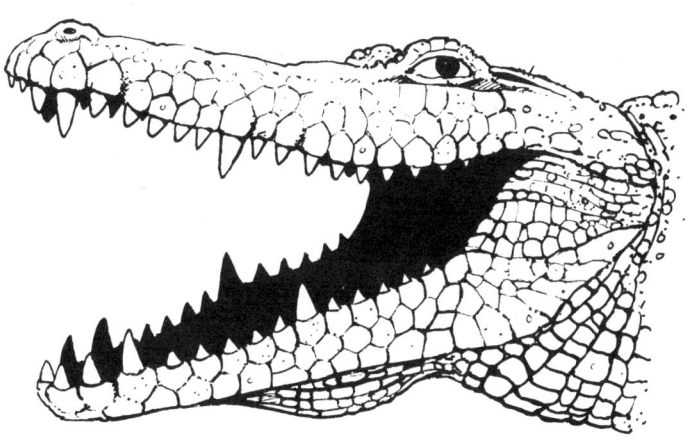

29

Peter shouted down that it didn't need a magic spell, though – all Wendy had to do was take another breath! So this was what Wendy did – and Peter was right – she continued to slide down! No sooner had she reached the underground home at the bottom, however, than she quickly started climbing up again. 'The boys have been kidnapped, Peter,' she told him with concern just as he was about to come down himself. 'Look – I found this note signed by Captain Hook. He says he has taken them off to his pirate ship!' Peter was quick to respond to the calamity, immediately instructing that they fly off in search of Captain Hook. John gave Wendy, Michael and himself another sprinkle of fairy dust to make sure they didn't flag in this important flight.

Remove a FAIRY DUST CARD from your TOP-HAT CARD. Now go to 98.

30

Wendy wanted to creep away from the redskin camp but Peter had other ideas. 'What about making an attack on them?' he suggested eagerly. 'All in favour, raise their hands!' Much to Wendy's horror, up shot John and Michael's hands and so it was to be an attack. But the children were heavily outnumbered and so it wasn't long before the redskins forced their surrender! ***Go to 200.***

Tinker Bell decided to fly at the front, thinking it only right since she had been flying for as long as she could remember. She certainly wasn't going to go behind children who had only just learnt! So they all followed her trail of light as it sparkled through the night sky. Just as the children's town was disappearing far behind them, however, Tinker Bell suddenly came to a halt, making them all bump into each other. She started gabbling away at Wendy, a fierce look in her eye. 'She's speaking in Neverlander,' Peter exclaimed when Wendy asked what she was saying. 'I'll see if I have my dictionary with me so you can translate.'

Do you have the NEVERLAND DICTIONARY CARD in the slit of your CHARACTER CARD? If so, use it to find out what Tinker Bell is saying by translating the instruction in her speech-balloon below. (Remember to return the NEVERLAND DICTIONARY to the CHARACTER CARD afterwards.) If you don't have one, go to 165 instead.

DIDDLY PUTT
ISH UCK SUL
WAP LIG

32

Suddenly, a strong gust of wind blew across the top of the cliffs, snatching John's hat off. 'The winds are a lot more playful here than where you come from,' Peter explained merrily as the hat tossed and turned in the air. 'They like to have some fun!' he added with a grin. John didn't consider it much fun, though, as he chased after his hat – especially since those precious pouches of fairy dust were inside! Finally, the wind grew bored with the game and dropped John's hat to the ground. John immediately checked inside to see if any of the pouches had burst. Unfortunately, one had!

Remove one of the FAIRY DUST CARDS from your TOP-HAT CARD. Now go to 197.

33

'I don't have a telescope,' Peter told her cheekily, 'so we'll just have to find them by exploring after all!' He added that the exploring didn't just have to be on foot, they could do some of it by flying as well. So it really would be quite fun! 'Well, all right then, Peter,' Wendy relented at last. 'But no more exploring than is absolutely necessary. And if there's going to be some more flying involved, you'd better wait a moment while John, Michael and I have another sprinkle of fairy dust. You can never be too prepared, you know!'

Remove one of the FAIRY DUST CARDS from your TOP-HAT CARD. Now go to 208.

34

'REALLY, Peter – you must tell Tinker Bell not to be so rude!' Wendy remarked indignantly when she had used the dictionary to translate what the fairy had said. Curious, Peter asked what it was exactly. 'Well,' Wendy began rather awkwardly, 'she said that it was a pity I didn't bruise myself somewhere rather more – er – delicate.' Wendy had expected Peter to be equally indignant at this but, much to her dismay, he gave out a peal of gleeful laughter! *Go to 103.*

35

Since he didn't have his telescope, Peter decided he would just have to fly up into the tree to find Tinker Bell. Eventually, he spotted her, and quickly grabbed her by the wings. 'Now, say you're sorry to Wendy!' he insisted as he brought her back down again. The mischievous fairy writhed and wriggled for all she was worth but she at last gave up. The faintest of tinkles from her was her rather grudging apology to Wendy. There was another humiliation for Tinker Bell because all that writhing and wriggling had sapped her strength and she could no longer fly. To show there was no ill feeling, Wendy gently sprinkled her with a pouch of fairy dust.

Remove one of the FAIRY DUST CARDS from your TOP-HAT-CARD. Now go to 61.

36

The children had now been captive aboard the pirates' ship for three long hours. 'We seem to have been sailing for miles,' moaned Michael. Nevertheless, this proved quite a good way of viewing Neverland because they witnessed many fantastic sights on their voyage. At this very moment, for instance, they were sailing past a bay where the sea was of seven different colours! 'It's called Rainbow Bay,' explained Peter, 'because they are the seven colours of the rainbow.' Wendy thought it would be a good idea to look it up on the map to find out exactly where they were. 'You do have your map, don't you Peter?' she asked warily.

Use your MAP to find which square Rainbow Bay is in – then follow the appropriate instruction. If you don't have one, you'll have to guess which instruction to follow.

If you think A1	go to 234
If you think B1	go to 136
If you think A2	go to 194

37

Peter didn't have his telescope, though! As a result, by the time the children had risen from the ground, the Never goose had disappeared. They therefore immediately came down to land again. Now that all their fairy dust pouches had gone, it was important to do as little flying as possible! 'Do you think we'll ever see my hat and the pouches again?' John asked as they walked dejectedly along. As a matter of fact, they *did* . . . because, some while later, they came across the hat sticking in some mud. 'The Never goose must have dropped it!' John cried joyously. It wasn't all joy, though, because one of the fairy dust pouches had split open!

Remove a FAIRY DUST CARD from your TOP-HAT CARD. Now go to 18. (Remember: when there are no FAIRY DUST CARDS left in your TOP-HAT CARD the game is over, and you must start again from the beginning.)

38

Our adventurers had left the cave some way behind when Peter asked if they had ever seen a polar bear. If not, he could take them to one! 'That would be perfectly delightful,' replied Wendy, 'but don't polar bears live in very cold parts, Peter? Surely there aren't any of those in Neverland?' But Peter told her that there were both very cold parts and very hot parts in Neverland – it was much more interesting that way! And just to prove it, he started leading them towards a cold part. 'You should be able to spot the icebergs very soon,' he said as they flew through the air.

Throw the special DICE to decide who is to spot the icebergs first.

PETER thrown	go to 236
TINKER BELL thrown	go to 96
WENDY thrown	go to 219
JOHN thrown	go to 19
MICHAEL thrown	go to 128
MAGIC thrown	go to 169

39

'She says she's crying because she's lost her reflection in the water,' Wendy explained to the others as she used their dictionary to translate what the mermaid was saying. The children all glanced down into the water and found that it was true. The mermaid's reflection wasn't there! 'Perhaps it's sunk to the bottom!' Peter suggested, and he immediately dived into the water, swimming for the seabed. Eventually he found the reflection, clinging to a rusty old anchor. As he brought it up again, the mermaid was so pleased that she gave him a Neverland map.

If you don't already have it there, put the MAP into your CHARACTER CARD. Now go to 28.

40

Some time after the children had left Mermaid Cove, they flew over a muddy creek. 'Let me introduce you to a crocodile!' Peter suggested breezily. The children weren't sure they wanted to be introduced to a crocodile but Peter was already leading the way down to the creek. 'It's usually round here somewhere,' Peter said when they had all come to land at the creek's edge. Wendy was just breathing a sigh of relief, thinking the crocodile had moved on, when a large green snout emerged from the muddy water. The crocodile then clambered up on to the mud. 'Quick, Peter!' Wendy cried as it started to approach them, its grin showing sharp teeth. 'Use your magic spell book to save us!'

Use your MAGIC SPELL BOOK to find the right spell used for this by placing exactly over the shape below – then follow the appropriate instruction. If you don't have one, you'll have to guess which instruction to follow.

If you think it's NIPPER	go to 85
If you think it's INCISOR	go to 129
If you think it's MOLAR	go to 9

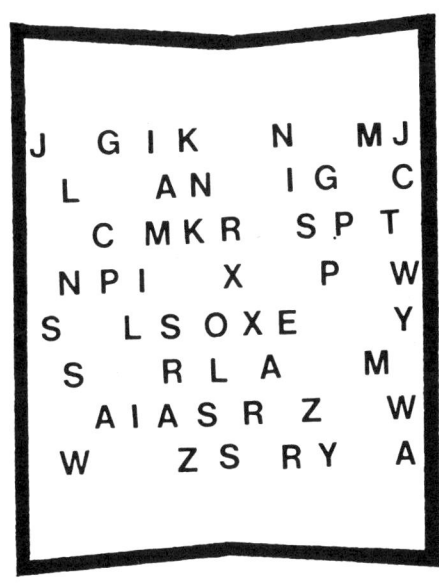

41

Wendy had just found Sunset Bay on Peter's map when little Michael gave a shriek! 'Look, there's a ticking crocodile in the bay!' he exclaimed. Wendy told him not to be so silly. There were hardly likely to be any crocodiles down there – and certainly not ones that ticked! Peter was to correct her, though, saying that there *was* a crocodile and it *did* tick! 'The ticking is made by an alarm clock it once swallowed,' he explained simply. 'But the crocodile is nothing to be afraid of. The only person it hungers for is the pirate, Captain Hook!' ***Go to 118.***

42

'It's written by the pirate, Captain Hook!' Peter exclaimed as they used his dictionary to translate the note. 'It says that he has kidnapped the boys and taken them to his ship as prisoners!' Peter realised that this was a trap, to lure *himself* on to Captain Hook's ship, but he was never one to be afraid of a challenge. So he immediately ordered that they fly off in search of the ship! Just as they were leaving the underground home, Wendy noticed a map on the floor. Assuming it to belong to one of the boys, she decided to take it with them.

If you don't already have it there, put the MAP into your CHARACTER CARD. Now go to 98.

Suddenly, Tinker Bell gave an excited tinkle and the others all looked beneath them. There was the waterfall! Not long after they had passed over it, they came to the blue expanse of the sea. But where was Captain Hook's ship? As they were scanning the horizon for it, Peter suddenly noticed a tiny rowing-boat bobbing up and down on the waves. And sat all alone in the boat was a fat little man with glasses. 'That's Smee, Captain Hook's bo'sun,' Peter told the others. 'He's the only one of Hook's crew with any heart!' As they flew nearer, they noticed that Smee was sobbing behind the glasses and Wendy gently asked him what was wrong. His reply was in Neverlander, though!

Use your NEVERLAND DICTIONARY to find out the reason for Smee's grief by translating the instruction in his speech-balloon below. If you don't have one, go to 276 instead.

> DIDDLY PUTT
> MELF YIK

44

John was by now becoming so fed up sitting in the crow's-nest that he decided to go and ask Captain Hook for another job. Rather than climbing all the way down, he thought it would be a lot quicker just to fly down. But he was just about to leap into the air when he suddenly realised that he might not have enough flying power. Imagine if he suddenly ran out halfway down and crashed to his doom! Just to be on the safe side, therefore, he gave himself a quick sprinkle with some more fairy dust.

Remove one of the FAIRY DUST CARDS from your TOP-HAT CARD. Now go to 77. (Remember: when there are no FAIRY DUST CARDS left in your TOP-HAT CARD the game is over, and you must start again from the beginning.)

45

Peter hadn't brought his telescope, though, and so they decided they would just have to land and make a thorough search of the ground. 'It's like looking for a needle in a haystack,' Wendy complained as they all felt around with their feet. Oddly, there *was* a haystack just a few metres in front of them and Peter thought searching for this needle Wendy was talking about might be more fun. He was sure *he* could find it! Well, he didn't but he *did* find the three pouches of fairy dust. Although, I suppose it was only two really . . . because the third, sadly, had burst.

Remove one of the FAIRY DUST CARDS from your TOP-HAT CARD. Now go to 132.

46

Michael reached Neverland first. It was more by accident than by skill, though, because he fell through the air much more quickly than he had wished. It all came of pointing his nose downward a bit *too* much – a fast way of descending, but not a very safe one! They found themselves near an old ruined castle on the cliff-tops. 'Isn't it spooky!' Wendy said nervously as she looked up at its gloomy turrets but Peter didn't know what *spooky* meant. He only saw things in terms of exciting adventures! 'Let's look up the castle on the map,' John suggested, 'and then we'll know exactly where we are in Neverland.'

Use your MAP to find which square the castle is in – then follow the appropriate instruction. If you don't have one, you'll have to guess which instruction to follow.

If you think A3	go to 143
If you think B3	go to 102
If you think B4	go to 2

47

Peter didn't have his magic spell book with him, though, and so didn't know which magic spell word to use. It didn't really matter, though, because the very next moment they found themselves landing *bump!* on one of Neverland's beautiful beaches. 'That's odd,' remarked Wendy, 'I don't remember spotting Neverland from afar.' Peter explained that the island probably spotted them, though, perhaps becoming a little impatient! ***Go to 103.***

48

It was exactly as Wendy had feared (and Peter had hoped!). The map showed that the home of the lost boys was at the very opposite end of the island. 'Well, we can just fly there *straight away*!' Wendy insisted but Peter told her it was impossible. In Neverland, you could only journey from one part to another by undergoing an adventure at each place – to make travelling much more exciting! ***Go to 208***.

49

John spotted an ice-cream tree first, pointing out a tree laden with chocolate-flavoured cornets to his left. At least, he assumed it was an ice-cream tree. He couldn't think what else it could be! When they had all stodged themselves on the ice-cream, they continued on their travels, eventually coming across a signpost. The directions were in Neverlander, though, and so they would need a dictionary to work them out.

Use your NEVERLAND DICTIONARY to read the signpost by translating the instruction below. If you don't have one, go to 281 instead.

DIDDLY PUTT
ISH UCK SUL WAP KER

50

Wailing Lake was only a short distance away, fortunately, and with the help of their map they soon reached it. They spotted Tiger Lily in the very middle of the lake; bound hand and foot on a tiny rock. 'The first downpour of rain and the poor thing will be drowned!' Wendy remarked, shaking her head at the pirates' cruelty. It was only a few brief moments, though, before Peter had dived into the water and cut Tiger Lily free. Tinker Bell observed his heroics with a certain irritation. Now he would have another female admirer! ***Go to 125.***

51

'He says he wants revenge because you cut off his right hand!' Wendy told Peter as, with the dictionary, she translated the Captain's address. She was rather shocked at this accusation. 'Oh, Peter, is it true – did you cut off his right hand?' she asked him disapprovingly. Peter proudly said it was true, though, and that he would do the same to the left one if he had the chance! ***Go to 36.***

52

Peter woke first, stretching his arms and eager for another day! The others were just awaking when three dark figures appeared at the entrance of the cave. They were witches! The children realised that they must have been sleeping in the witches' house while they were out for the night, doing their evil deeds. 'They look rather angry with us, don't they?' Michael said as the witches started to cackle hideously. Suddenly, one of them shook her long, bony fingers at Michael and he immediately turned into a frog! 'Oh, poor Michael!' wailed Wendy. 'Quick, Peter, use your magic spell book to reverse the spell and change him back again!'

Use your MAGIC SPELL BOOK to find the right spell word for this by placing exactly over the shape below – then follow the appropriate instruction. If you don't have one, you'll have to guess which instruction to follow.

If you think it's SORCERY	go to 201
If you think it's CAULDRON	go to 245
If you think it's BROOMSTICK	go to 137

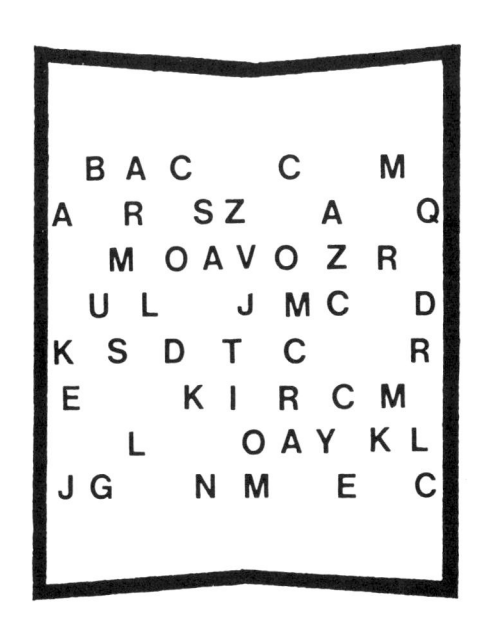

```
B A C     C      M
A  R  S Z   A      Q
   M O A V O Z R
   U L    J M C    D
K  S D T C          R
E      K I R C M
    L      O A Y K L
J G    N M    E    C
```

53

'He's asking us if we would like to come to their igloo for a nice warm-up and some charcoal-baked fish,' Wendy translated as the Eskimo repeated his words. She immediately flicked through the dictionary for the Neverland for 'thank you, we would be delighted'. The Eskimoes then led them to their igloo. It wasn't a normal one like Wendy had seen in her picture books, but a multi-coloured one. The blocks of ice that formed the walls were every shade you could think of: some orange, some green, some purple! It was at last time for the children to leave the igloo, the Eskimoes giving them a map as a present as they exchanged farewells.

If you don't already have it there, put the MAP into your CHARACTER CARD. Now go to 181.

54

'Oh, Peter!' Wendy declared with dismay as she used the dictionary to translate the penguin's squawks. 'It's saying that they don't want you here because you once teased them for having such silly little wings. I can't believe you did – did you?' she asked with concern. Peter had a think for a moment, scratching his head. The truth was he simply couldn't remember! 'Well, I'm sure you *weren't* that horrible,' Wendy said, giving him the benefit of the doubt, but she soon began to wonder. For, as the children now flew up into the sky, Wendy noticed that Peter was making a great show of his flying ability. Was it to tease the penguins yet again? ***Go to 109.***

55

Michael entered the tree first, crawling through a large squirrel-hole. After he had slid down, in just the way Peter had instructed, John took his turn . . . then Wendy, then Peter, then Tinker Bell. When they had all reached the underground home at the bottom, however, they found that it was empty! 'Perhaps the lost boys are out hunting somewhere,' Peter suggested and so he started climbing the tree again, climbing and climbing, until he reached the very top this time. There, he popped his head out, searching all round for the boys. He reached under his belt for his telescope to make his search easier.

Use your TELESCOPE to try and spot the lost boys by placing exactly over the shape below – then follow the instruction. If you don't have one, go to 259 instead.

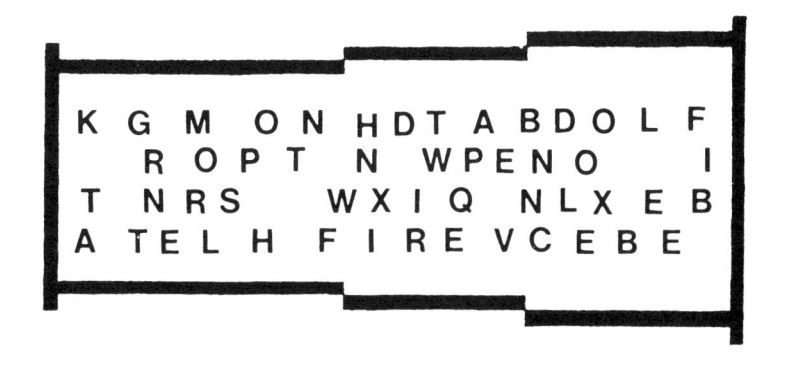

```
K  G  M   O N  H DT  A  B D O   L  F
   R  O P T    N   W P E N O           I
T  N R S       W X I Q    N L X   E  B
A   T E L  H   F  I R E  V C  E B  E
```

56

'The lost boys have been kidnapped and taken away!' Wendy exclaimed with horror as she used Peter's dictionary to translate what the tree was saying. She asked it who the kidnapper was but the poor tree was much too upset to answer. It just shed leaf after leaf

on to the ground! 'I know who it is!' Peter cried, suddenly noticing a map near his feet. 'This map has the name of Captain Hook, the pirate, on it. He must have taken the lost boys away to his ship!' Tucking the map under his belt, he immediately ordered them all to prepare to fly off in search of Captain Hook!

If you don't already have it there, put the MAP into your CHARACTER CARD. Now go to 98.

57

Peter began to weep even louder, though, telling Wendy that he could only magic Tinker Bell better with the right spell word – and he had forgotten to bring his magic spell book with him! Suddenly, though, he began to cheer up, remembering another way to bring dead fairies back to life again. 'All you have to do is say that you believe in them,' he told the children. Wendy, John and Michael said that of course they believed in fairies . . . and, suddenly, Tinker Bell was right as rain again! *Go to 123.*

58

Peter insisted that he should fly at the front, outraged at the thought that anyone else should be their leader! 'Well, as you will, Peter,' Wendy conceded, sounding rather motherly, 'but don't think that you're always to do the leading on this adventure. There are others to consider, you know.' Peter gave a scowl at her gentle chiding, wondering whether mothers were such a good thing after all. He had only just got up a bit of speed when Wendy annoyed him again. She was tugging at his ankles, suddenly ordering him to stop. 'There are two people down there waving their arms at us,' she cried. 'I wonder if it's mother and father!' She asked Peter if he had a telescope so she could check.

Do you have the TELESCOPE CARD in the slit of your CHARACTER CARD? If so, use it to find out who is doing the waving by placing exactly over the shape below – then follow the instruction. (Remember to return the TELESCOPE to the CHARACTER CARD afterwards.) If you don't have one, go to 278 instead.

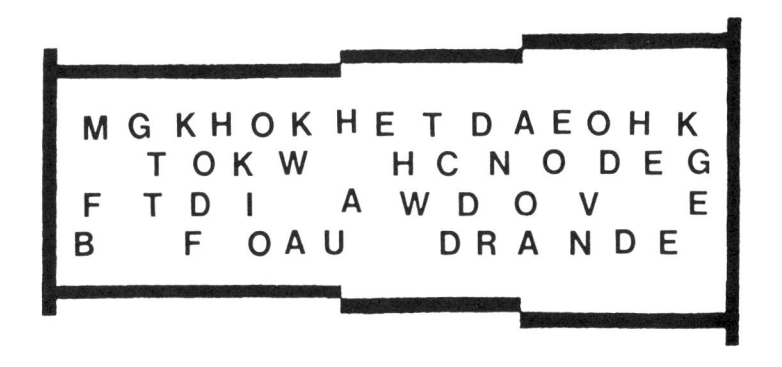

```
M G K H O K   H E T   D A E O H K
   T O K W       H C N   O D E G
F  T D I      A   W D O V       E
B    F   O A U       D R A N D E
```

59
'It says *WELCOME TO NEVERLAND!*' Wendy translated the sign as soon as Peter had handed her his dictionary. John asked how it was that the sign knew the exact point that they would land. 'Signs are different in Neverland,' Peter explained simply. 'Where you come from, people have to go and find the signs. In Neverland, though, the signs go and find the people. It's much less bother that way.' John had a think about this for a moment. Yes, he had to admit, it was! *Go to 197.*

60

'He's telling us that he's having his lunch and that he doesn't want to be disturbed!' Wendy told the others as she used the dictionary to translate what the gnome was saying. She now noticed the little packet of sandwiches at the gnome's side, feeling rather bad about it. 'Oh, I'm very sorry – I didn't realise!' she apologised. This seemed to make the gnome rather more amenable for he suddenly produced a map from under his tunic, handing it to them. 'This is obviously to help us find the lost boys' home!' she exclaimed to the others.

If you don't already have it there, put the MAP into your CHARACTER CARD. Now go to 208.

61

Peter and the children hadn't travelled much further through Neverland when Wendy suddenly spotted some puffs of smoke in the distance. 'What are they?' she asked curiously as the puffs rose one after the other into the sky. 'They're smoke signals!' Peter exclaimed with delight. 'There must be a redskin camp behind that mountain. Quick, let's fly over to it and see what they're up to!'

Throw the special DICE to decide who is to reach the redskin camp first.

PETER thrown	go to 217
TINKER BELL thrown	go to 282
WENDY thrown	go to 135
JOHN thrown	go to 255
MICHAEL thrown	go to 16
MAGIC thrown	go to 178

62

'He's telling us that we are to be taken aboard his ship and press-ganged into being pirates,' Wendy said as she used the dictionary to translate the Captain's words. Wendy showed a certain haughty disdain for the idea but John and Michael were rather thrilled by it. 'Does that mean we'll never have to wash behind our ears again?' Michael asked enthusiastically as they were escorted into a little rowing-boat and rowed out to the waiting *Jolly Roger*. 'No, it certainly does not!' Wendy rebuked him firmly. ***Go to 158.***

In actual fact, Peter, Tinker Bell and the children all woke exactly together! This was because in Neverland it is possible to share the same dream. And if the dream is the same, then of course it will end at exactly the same time. 'I had a dream all about yellow elephants,' said Michael, who did not really understand about shared dreams. 'Yes, they were rather cute, weren't they?' came the casual response of Peter, who knew all about them! They were just starting to think about breakfast when a wolf appeared at the cave's entrance! It started to howl something at them and so Wendy quickly asked Peter for his dictionary to work out what it was saying.

*Use your **NEVERLAND DICTIONARY** to make sense of the wolf's howls by translating the instruction in its speech-balloon below. If you don't have one, go to 87 instead.*

> DIDDLY PUTT
> ISH UCK SUL
> WAP BLIP

64

'*MISCHIEF!*' Wendy declared, almost in tears, and suddenly her hair changed back to its beautiful colour again. The mermaids were in such a mood at this that they swam off to another rock, well away from Peter and the children. There, they furiously combed at their hair, combing and combing until it gleamed in the sun. They then held up a mirror for each other, no doubt telling themselves that Wendy's hair was not nearly as luxurious as theirs after all! ***Go to 28.***

65

'What do we do now?' Wendy exclaimed with horror as Peter confessed that he had forgotten his magic spell book, but John was already taking action. He whipped a fairy dust pouch from under his top-hat and swooped down after Michael. Just as Michael was about to drop between the crocodile's eager, wide-open jaws, John showered him with the dust. It immediately took effect and Michael started to flap upwards again. But some of the dust had fallen on the crocodile as well and there was a moment of alarm as it flew up after Michael. Fortunately, though, it was only a very small amount – the bewildered crocodile soon came to a halt and crashed back into the water again!

Remove one of the FAIRY DUST CARDS from your TOP-HAT CARD. Now go to 118. (Remember: when there are no FAIRY DUST CARDS left in your TOP-HAT CARD the game is over, and you must start again from the beginning.)

66

Michael spotted the waterfall first – and shortly after that our adventurers arrived at the sea. But finding the vast expanse of the sea was one thing, finding Hook's ship was another! 'It must be down there *somewhere*!' said Wendy as they all shielded their eyes. They were still squinting and searching when a strange-looking bird came flapping past them. It was a Never bird and Wendy had the wonderful idea of asking if *it* had seen Captain Hook's ship. The Never bird seemed to understand Wendy's question all right but its reply, unfortunately, came in Neverlander!

Use your NEVERLAND DICTIONARY to make sense of the Never bird's reply by translating the instruction below. If you don't have one, go to 220 instead.

DIDDLY PUTT
ISH UCK SUL
LOD YIK

67

Since Peter didn't have his telescope, they just had to count the redskins as best they could. 'I make it thirteen,' said Wendy, but Peter made it ten. Wendy worked out that the average of the two was eleven and a half and, since this was under a dozen, she kept to her word and allowed the attack to go ahead. They therefore swooped down right into the middle of the redskin camp but they soon discovered that there were in fact thirteen of them there and the children were overpowered. One of the redskins tried to take John's scalp by sinking a tomahawk into his top-hat. The tomahawk just missed John, fortunately, but it did slice through one of the fairy dust pouches!

Remove one of the FAIRY DUST CARDS from your TOP-HAT CARD. Now go to 200.

68

Checking under his belt for his dictionary, Peter found that he had been forgetful there as well, though! 'First you forget how to speak your own language,' Wendy chided him with a little wag of her finger, 'then you forget your dictionary . . . just what will it be next, I wonder? Let's hope it's not how to fly or you'll be in a right pickle!' So the children could do nothing but wave the Never horse goodbye and continue on their flight. *Go to 132.*

69

Tinker Bell reached Neverland first, determined to impress Peter. Far from being impressed, though, Peter was annoyed that she hadn't let *him* win the race! 'You know I always like to come first!' he told her sulkily. Anyway, Peter's spirits soon lifted as he glanced round his beloved homeland again. 'I wonder if Captain Hook's anywhere nearby?' he asked excitedly as he looked out over the brilliant blue sea. He thought he could just discern his ship on the horizon – but he would need a telescope to make sure!

Use your TELESCOPE to find out whether it is Captain Hook's ship by placing exactly over the shape below – then follow the instruction. If you don't have one, go to 3 instead.

```
A G C E O   G K T M R   O T   W
  K T P T W W T O R N E     T
  H T L H  W R O E         E      F
H T  N  H A I D R D N F  E D E B
```

70

Peter didn't have a map, though, and so it looked as if he was going to get his own way after all. The only way they were going to be able to find the home of the lost boys was by doing some adventuring and exploring! 'Well, I insist we *fly* as much of the journey as possible!' Wendy declared, and she sprinkled herself and her two brothers with a pouch of fairy dust in preparation.

Remove one of the *FAIRY DUST CARDS* from your *TOP-HAT CARD*. Now go to 208.

71

Peter didn't have his magic spell book with him, though, and so that was the end of that idea! The pirates now made the children walk towards their ship, *Jolly Roger*, which was moored just around the corner. As John was being pushed along the boarding plank, he suddenly lost his footing. Fortunately, one of the pirates caught him before he fell into the water but his top-hat wobbled on his head as he stumbled . . . and out dropped one of his fairy dust pouches. It quickly sank to the bottom of the sea!

Remove one of the *FAIRY DUST CARDS* from your *TOP-HAT CARD*. Now go to 158.

72

Michael spotted a mermaid first. At least, he thought it was a mermaid – he couldn't think what else had beautiful blonde hair and a silvery tail! After the others had confirmed that it was indeed a mermaid, they all flew down to speak to her. She was sitting on a rock but as the children approached, they saw that she was sobbing. Little diamond tears dropped on to her small, bare shoulders. 'Why are you crying, mermaid?' Wendy asked gently but the mermaid's sniffed reply was in Neverlander, and so it was a job for their dictionary!

Use your NEVERLAND DICTIONARY to find out what the mermaid was saying by translating the instruction in her speech-balloon below. If you don't have one, go to 180 instead.

DIDDLY PUTT ONG YIK

73

The children hadn't been in the iceberg region long when they encountered that polar bear they had come to see. 'Isn't it lovely?' Wendy exclaimed with delight as it basked in the winter sun. 'It looks so cuddly just like a large white teddy bear!' Peter frowned at this, though, not knowing what a teddy bear was. 'Have you never had a teddy bear, Peter?' Wendy asked sympathetically. 'Well, never mind, as soon as we reach the lost boys' home, I'll make you one!' ***Go to 181.***

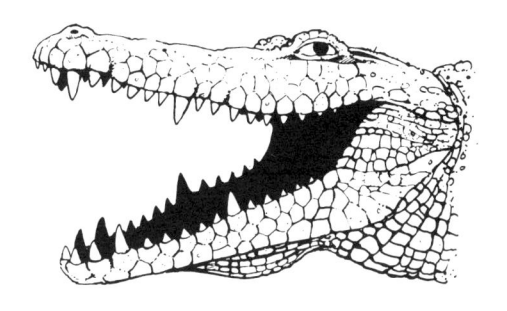

74

When it became time to depart from Crocodile Creek, Michael and John found that they could barely leave the ground. They flapped and flapped but the most they could manage was a couple of centimetres or so! The problem was those sausages. They had eaten so many that they were now much too heavy to fly. John had to empty a whole pouch of fairy dust over them both to correct the situation.

Remove a FAIRY DUST CARD from your TOP-HAT CARD. Now go to 118. (Remember: when there are no FAIRY DUST CARDS left in your TOP-HAT CARD the game is over, and you must start again from the beginning.)

Wendy was so impatient to meet the lost boys at last that *she* asked if she might enter the tree first. So she crawled through a large squirrel-hole in the tree, taking a breath exactly as Peter had instructed. She immediately began to slide down but it was further than she had expected and she hadn't taken a deep enough breath. She simply couldn't help breathing out again! 'Oh, Peter, I'm stuck!' she called up as she came to a sudden halt. 'See if there's a spell in your magic spell book to make me grow thinner!'

Use your MAGIC SPELL BOOK to find the right word for this by placing exactly over the shape below – then follow the appropriate instruction. If you don't have one, you'll have to guess which instruction to follow.

      If you think it's SPINDLY   go to 29
      If you think it's BEANPOLE   go to 182
      If you think it's SKINNY   go to 110

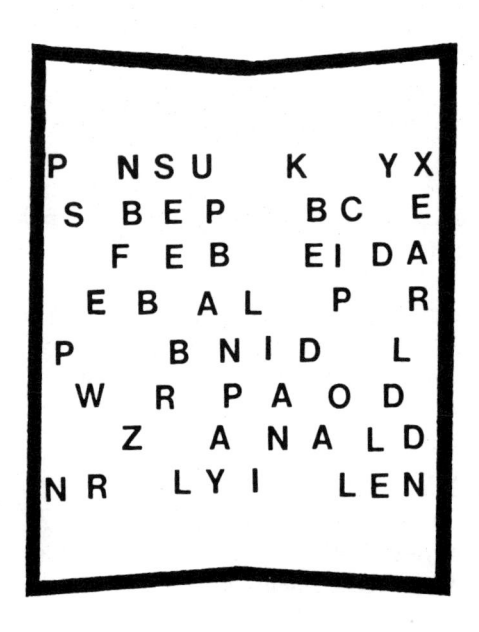

```
P   N S U      K     Y X
  S B E P      B C     E
    F E B      E I D A
    E B A L      P     R
P     B N I D         L
  W   R  P A O D
      Z   A N A L D
N R     L Y I     L E N
```

76

Blushing, Peter discovered he had forgotten his telescope, though! The boys therefore decided just to tear off bits of the candyfloss cloud with their hands – but they were soon to regret their decision. For their hands became so sticky that it affected their flying! As the iceberg region at last appeared below, John and Michael started to tumble about all over the place. In fact, it looked as if they might well land on that hard ice head first! So John quickly sprinkled them both with a pouch of fairy dust to help them regain control.

Remove one of the FAIRY DUST CARDS from your TOP-HAT CARD. Now go to 181.

77

The pirate ship sailed on and on but then a storm suddenly arose, forcing it into the treacherous rocks off the shore. Captain Hook desperately called every hand on deck to try and save his beloved vessel. Through luck more than skill, the ship just managed to survive and the storm finally began to subside. But when the Captain went to check on his prisoners, he found that they had all gone. Peter, Tinker Bell and the children had quietly flown ashore during the turmoil! ***Go to 18.***

78

The children now started climbing the hollow tree to the outside again, so they could fly off in pursuit of Captain Hook's ship. But as John crawled out of the tree, his top-hat became wedged. A good tug from him brought it loose again . . . but it also made one of the fairy dust pouches fall out! He had to slide all the way down to the bottom of the tree to retrieve it. It proved a wasted journey, though, because the pouch had ripped open in the fall and the fairy dust was now fast vanishing in the air!

Remove one of the FAIRY DUST CARDS from your TOP-HAT CARD. Now go to 98.

79

'I do believe that is it, down there!' John suddenly remarked as he spotted a shimmering, beautiful island below. Peter confirmed that it was, giving a little gleeful spin in the air. He was all for making a landing right away but Wendy reminded him that, although she was quite used to *flying* by now, she had never done a *landing* before.

'So, I want you to pick out somewhere that's nice and soft,' she told him. 'Perhaps you could look through your telescope!'

Use your TELESCOPE to find a soft landing-place on the island by placing exactly over the shape below – then follow the instruction. If you don't have one, go to 23 instead.

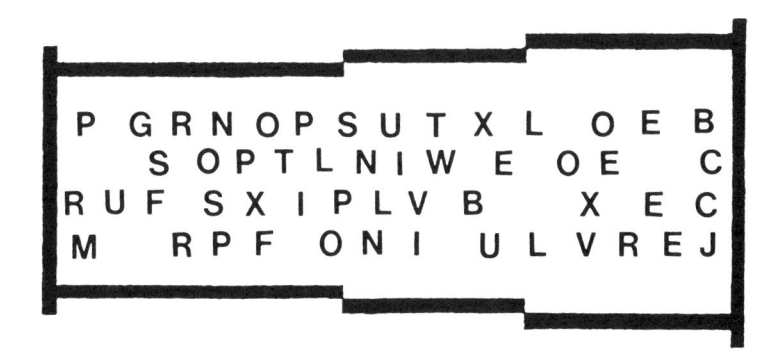

```
P   G R N O P S U T X L   O E   B
    S O P T L N I W   E   O E     C
R U F   S X I P L V   B       X   E C
M     R P F   O N I     U L V R E J
```

80

'I'm afraid I won't be able to magic one of the lost boys here after all,' Peter told Wendy bashfully when he discovered he didn't have his magic spell book with him. 'Well, then, we'd better start making a move right away,' Wendy said. 'And if you must have some adventures on the way, Peter, please make sure they are not too many. I really would like to reach the lost boys in time to give them their supper!' **Go to 208.**

81

As soon as Peter had uttered the magic word *SPARKLE*, all the ice-creams suddenly turned to chocolate flavour! 'Now don't eat too many or you'll make yourself fat!' Wendy warned him as he plucked one cornet after another. But her words were in vain because when Peter at last decided to fly down from the tree, he found that he dropped like a stone instead! 'I would have been all right if I wasn't carrying *this*!' Peter insisted, showing them a telescope he had found up in the tree.

If you don't already have it there, put the TELESCOPE CARD into your CHARACTER CARD. Now go to 61.

82

The pirates captured Michael first because deep down they were a rather cowardly lot and Michael was the smallest. Well, really Tinker Bell was the smallest but she flitted about a bit too much and looked difficult to catch. Anyway, they did finally capture them all and led them away towards their waiting ship. When the ship had sailed a good way out to sea, Captain Hook made them all stand in an orderly row while he addressed them. His speech was in Neverlander, though, and so Wendy asked Peter if he had a dictionary with him so they could understand it.

Use your NEVERLAND DICTIONARY to find out what

Captain Hook is saying by translating the instruction in his speech-balloon below. If you don't have one, go to 249 instead.

DIDDLY PUTT WAP LIG

83

Although Peter didn't have a telescope, he didn't need one – because the pirates' ship suddenly came into view ahead. There was a huge skull and crossbones flying from its mast! As the pirates made the children board the ship, one of them roughly knocked John's hat off. Seeing the pouches of fairy dust inside, he greedily opened one up, assuming it contained gold. When he discovered it didn't, he angrily dashed the dust into John's face. Of course, John didn't mind because it meant that he now had some more flying power . . . but it also meant that he had one pouch less!

Remove one of the FAIRY DUST CARDS from your TOP-HAT CARD. Now go to 158.

84

The children hadn't left the witches' cave far behind when Peter suggested paying a visit to Mermaid Cove. Wendy reminded him that they were meant to be travelling to the lost boys but she had to admit that Peter's suggestion had a certain appeal. 'Are there real mermaids there,' she asked, fascinated, 'with real tails and golden hair?' Peter said that of course there were mermaids there and so Wendy was won over. 'After all, we've got a whole day ahead of us,' she said as they began to head towards Mermaid Cove. They at last arrived there, landing on the cliff-top above. 'Look very carefully,' Peter said, pointing down into the sea, 'and you should be able to see one!'

Throw the special DICE to decide who is to spot a mermaid first.

PETER thrown	go to 247
TINKER BELL thrown	go to 160
WENDY thrown	go to 258
JOHN thrown	go to 184
MICHAEL thrown	go to 72
MAGIC thrown	go to 210

85

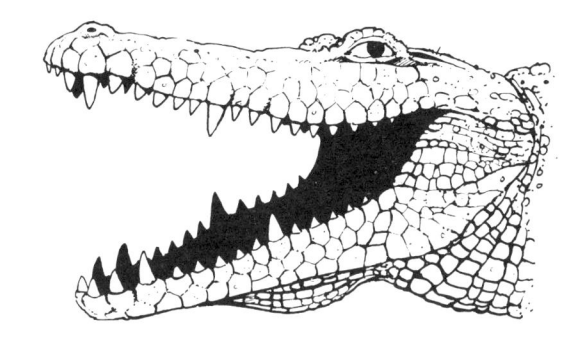

Since Peter didn't have his magic spell book, all the children shut their eyes, preparing themselves for their doom. Wendy braced herself as she felt the crocodile's snout touch her bare toes. But it didn't seem to fancy Wendy and moved on to the others. They weren't to the crocodile's taste either though, and so, disappointedly, it returned to the water. Suddenly, Peter remembered about the crocodile, realising the reason for this. 'I once fed it Captain Hook's right hand after I sliced it off,' he told the others. 'The crocodile liked the flavour of the captain so much that it now turns its snout up at almost everybody else!' ***Go to 118.***

86

They were just about to leave Sunset Bay when Peter asked the children if they would like to see a crocodile. He then led the way down to the water, hovering just above its surface. 'Ahoy, shipmates!' he cried at the top of his voice and suddenly a large green snout appeared, full of razor-sharp teeth! 'It thinks I'm the pirate, Captain Hook,' Peter giggled as the snout chased him around, trying to snap at his heels. 'You see, after I cut Hook's right hand off in a duel, I threw it to the crocodile for his dinner. He liked it so

much that now he spends all his time trying to find the rest of him!'
The children thought this game of teasing the crocodile was a bit too dangerous, though, and so John sprinkled them all with a pouch of fairy dust to make sure they could fly well away from those snapping jaws.

Remove one of the FAIRY DUST CARDS from your TOP-HAT CARD. Now go to 118. (Remember: when there are no FAIRY DUST CARDS left in your TOP-HAT CARD the game is over, and you must start again from the beginning.)

87

Although Peter didn't have his dictionary, he could have a pretty good guess at what the wolf was trying to say! He was telling them that the cave belonged to *him* and that they had no right to trespass there. So the children hastily gathered their things together, ready to leave. In John's case, though, it was a bit too hasty because he overlooked one of the fairy dust pouches as he was scooping them back into his hat!

Remove one of the FAIRY DUST CARDS from your TOP-HAT CARD. Now go to 38.

88

Peter discovered that he had forgotten his telescope, and so he couldn't be sure whether the lost boys were on deck or not. 'Well, we'll find out soon enough!' he said as he now swooped down on the pirate ship. The children followed him a cautious distance behind. No sooner had they alighted on the ship than Peter called out Hook's name, demanding that he draw out his sword. 'It's you or me this time, Hook!' he cried. As the fight between the two arch-foes commenced, John sprinkled Wendy, Michael and himself with another pouch of fairy dust. Should Peter lose the duel, he wanted to be sure of a swift escape!

Remove a FAIRY DUST CARD from your TOP-HAT CARD. Now go to 11. (Remember: when there are no FAIRY DUST CARDS left in your TOP-HAT CARD the game is over, and you must start again.)

89

'He says he's been marooned,' Wendy told the others as she used Peter's dictionary to translate what Smee was sobbing about. 'It was because Hook caught him trying to help the lost boys escape!' Wendy was so touched by this little man's humanity and heroism that she promised that she would be *his* mother too! For the moment, though, they had to take their leave of the bo'sun because there was still that ship to be found. At last they spotted it and Peter led the swoop down with a gallant cry. 'Hook!' he yelled at his arch-enemy as he drew out his sword. 'It's you or me this time!' *Go to 11.*

90

'Oh, Peter, you are forgetful!' Wendy chided him when he confessed that he had left his dictionary back at their house. Since they couldn't work out what the book was, there didn't seem much point in taking it, and so she carefully placed it back in the grass. She rather suspected it might belong to fairies! ***Go to 253.***

91

Although Peter didn't have a telescope, he said he could quite easily guess who had fired the cannonball. 'It's Captain Hook, I expect,' he told them airily, 'my arch-enemy!' He explained that Captain Hook was a pirate and that his ship terrorised the seas off Neverland. 'A pirate! How wonderful!' John and Michael both exclaimed with delight – but it was a delight Wendy did not share. 'Oh dear, I do hope we don't have too much trouble from him!' she said anxiously as they all finally landed on Neverland. ***Go to 123.***

92

Since Peter didn't have his magic spell book, it looked as if they would just have to fly down after all. Peter went first, rather showing off as he did so. Instead of flying down nicely and safely, he dropped like a stone – only flapping his arms at the very last moment, just before he hit the ground. He tried to coax the others to do the same but Wendy would have none of it. 'This sort of showing off will only end in tears, Peter,' she told him sternly as she led her two brothers in a much more responsible descent. ***Go to 197.***

93

Although Michael had never seen an ice-cream tree before, he had a pretty good picture in his mind of what one would look like! 'There's one!' he cried, as he suddenly spotted a sort of apple tree. The only difference was that, instead of growing apples, it grew vanilla cornets! After they had plucked as many ice-creams as they could carry, they flew to the nearest beach to eat them. 'It looks like a smugglers' beach,' John said excitedly as he noticed the two large caves there and the dozens upon dozens of rum barrels. He asked Peter if he had his map so they could look it up.

Use your MAP to find which square the smugglers' beach is in – then follow the appropriate instruction. If you don't have one, you'll have to guess which instruction to follow.

If you think B4	go to 12
If you think C4	go to 124
If you think D4	go to 216

94

John was by now feeling so giddy sitting in the crow's-nest that he decided to go and ask Captain Hook if someone else could have a turn. It would have been a lot easier just to fly down to him but John was concerned that he might not have enough flying power. He could always give himself another sprinkle of fairy dust, of course, but he didn't really want to waste the pouches. So – very selflessly – he began the long, dizzy clamber down! **Go to 77.**

95

Since Peter didn't have a telescope, John volunteered to fly across to the battle. 'I'll come back with my report as soon as possible!' he told them as he set off eagerly. When John did eventually return, however, it was in the hands of the pirates! 'I'm afraid *they* won!' he said as the pirates now captured the rest of the children and forced them aboard their ship. As the ship set sail, John had some more bad news to relate. He had spilt one of his pouches of fairy dust when the pirates had captured him!

Remove one of the FAIRY DUST CARDS from your TOP-HAT CARD. Now go to 36.

96

A determined tinkle from her showed that *Tinker Bell* had spotted the icebergs first. She didn't want any of the others claiming the achievement! As they came down to land on one of the flatter icebergs, a number of penguins swam towards them. They eased themselves up on to the ice in that funny way of theirs and then came waddling around the children. The biggest penguin started squawking at them but its squawks were in Neverlander and so they would need a dictionary to make any sense of them!

Use your NEVERLAND DICTIONARY to find out what the penguin was saying by translating the instruction in its speech-balloon below. If you don't have one, go to 248 instead.

DIDDLY PUTT WAP KER

97

Wendy gasped in horror as Peter confessed that he had forgotten his magic spell book. 'Oh, poor Michael,' she cried, 'the crocodile will gobble him up!' But Peter told her that Michael would be perfectly safe because the crocodile had an appetite solely for Captain Hook. It had liked his right hand so much that it wouldn't even consider any other flavour. And so it proved because, when Michael landed on the crocodile's snout, it simply tossed him back into the air again! ***Go to 118.***

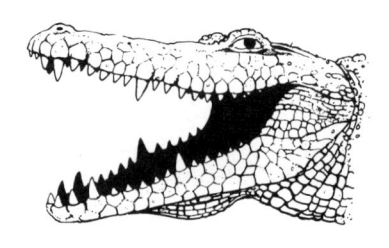

98

Peter and the children flapped their arms for all they were worth, knowing that there wasn't a moment to lose. Normally, they would just glide along in the air currents but this was no time for casual flying. 'The shortest way to the sea is via the high waterfall,' said Peter as he led the way . . .

Throw the special DICE to decide who is to spot the waterfall first.

PETER thrown	go to 229
TINKER BELL thrown	go to 43
WENDY thrown	go to 250
JOHN thrown	go to 268
MICHAEL thrown	go to 66
MAGIC thrown	go to 203

99

Since the children couldn't make any sense of what the mermaid was saying, they decided they had best leave her be. They were just about to fly off when the mermaid dived into the water, knocking off John's hat with her tail. He was sure it was deliberate! But deliberate or not, the hat half-filled with water as it rocked on the sea. One of the fairy dust pouches inside became so damp that the contents lost all its magic!

Remove one of the FAIRY DUST CARDS from your TOP-HAT CARD. Now go to 40.

100

Since Peter didn't have a dictionary with him, they decided they would just have to leave the sign as it was – untranslated! Wendy was sure that if Peter really put his mind to it he could remember some Neverlander *without* a dictionary. But all Peter seemed interested in was starting some adventure and so she knew there wasn't much hope. Their first adventure in fact began very quickly because Wendy suddenly slipped over the cliff's edge, and was only saved from the fierce sea below by a piece of frantic flying. It took so much out of her that she thought she'd better have another sprinkle of fairy dust to restore her power!

Remove one of the FAIRY DUST CARDS from your TOP-HAT CARD. Now go to 197.

Before they could agree who was to fly at the front, though, a winged horse suddenly appeared before them. 'Oh, it's called a Never horse,' Peter explained casually to the dumbfounded children. 'It must have decided to go for a bit of a roam.' Not only could this magical horse fly but the children discovered it could also talk! It was in a strange language, though, and they couldn't understand what it was trying to tell them. 'I expect it's Neverlander,' Peter said, not sounding at all guilty that he had so quickly forgotten his native tongue. 'I'll see if I have my Neverland dictionary with me!'

Do you have the NEVERLAND DICTIONARY CARD in the slit of your CHARACTER CARD? If so, use it to find out what the Never horse is saying by translating the instruction in its speech-balloon below. (Remember to return the NEVERLAND DICTIONARY to the CHARACTER CARD afterwards.) If you don't have one, go to 68 instead.

DIDDLY PUTT ISH UCK SUL LOD DINK

102

At the very moment Peter looked under his belt to see if he had a map, though, a fearsome singing sound came from across the water. 'Is it a ghost?' Michael asked nervously but Peter said it was much, much worse. 'It's the singing of Captain Hook's crew,' he told them. Wendy asked who this Captain Hook was. 'The most terrible pirate there ever was,' he replied. 'And my arch-enemy!' he added proudly. *Go to 123.*

103

'Right, let's begin our adventures!' Peter said eagerly, anxious not to waste any time. Wendy asked him what adventures he was talking about, though. 'I thought we'd come here so I could be mother to the lost boys,' she said. Peter then told her the problem – he couldn't remember where on the island the lost boys were. For all he knew, they could be a hundred – maybe even a thousand – adventures away! Wendy was really having none of this nonsense, though. She asked Peter what the home of the lost boys looked like so they could find it on the map. 'It's a group of trees,' Peter replied. 'They live underneath them, squeezing through little doors in their trunks!'

Use your MAP to find which square the home of the lost boys is in – then follow the appropriate instruction. If you don't have one, you'll have to guess which instruction to follow.

If you think D1	go to 48
If you think E1	go to 144
If you think E2	go to 70

104

Peter told Wendy that he didn't have his telescope – and he didn't need one either! 'I'm not scared of any silly old dragon!' he said, boldly marching into the cave's dark interior. Frightened that Peter might forget to come back to them, the children decided that they had better follow him. The cave went on and on, twisting and turning, but at last it emerged onto a sandy beach. 'Thank goodness!' exclaimed Wendy with relief. John had some bad news for her, though. His hat had been knocked off at a very low part of the cave and one of his pouches of fairy dust had spilt!

Remove one of the FAIRY DUST CARDS from your TOP-HAT CARD. Now go to 176.

105

Since they didn't have a dictionary, there was no way of telling what horror the chief had in store for them. And you can hardly fear what you can't make sense of . . . and so all their anxiety went. Highly impressed by this apparent courage of theirs, the chief decided to give them a reprieve. Just in case he changed his mind, the children prepared to fly off straight away. John quickly sprinkled Wendy, Michael and himself with a pouch of fairy dust to make sure they had enough power.

Remove one of the FAIRY DUST CARDS from your TOP-HAT CARD. Now go to 125.

106

Wendy woke first – so she could give the cave a good clean before the others woke up. As luck had it, there was a broom resting in the corner and she started to sweep the floor with it. She was just wondering how the broom had got there when some hideous old women appeared at the cave's entrance. They were witches! They started to croak something at her but their croaks were in Neverlander and so Wendy quickly woke Peter to borrow his dictionary.

Use your NEVERLAND DICTIONARY to find out what the

witches were saying by translating the instruction in their speech-balloon below. If you don't have one, go to 227 instead.

> DIDDLY PUTT
> LIG UCK SUL
> HO FLOM

107

'*MUSHROOM!*' the children shouted hungrily when they had found the right spell word in Peter's book . . . and breakfast miraculously appeared! I shan't tell you what it was in case it makes you hungry yourself but suffice to say that it was perfectly delicious. When they had all finished, Wendy hoped the same magic spell word could be used to do the washing-up. 'Mushroom,' she said expectantly but the dishes remained just as they were. She would just have to do them herself! ***Go to 38.***

108

Although Peter didn't have his magic spell book, he was determined Wendy's hair should be turned golden again. He didn't like it green any more than she did! So he quickly grabbed hold of one of the mermaids, threatening to tie her hair into such tight knots that she would never be able to comb them out again! The mermaid gasped in horror at the very thought and quickly reversed the spell on Wendy's hair. It became as beautifully golden as it was before! ***Go to 28.***

109

Some time after they had left the region of icebergs and polar bears, the children flew over a beautiful sandy bay. 'It will be growing dark again soon,' remarked Wendy, as streaks of red light rippled upon the water. 'Look, the sun's setting across the bay.' Peter gave a little giggle, though, and explained that the sun was *always* setting across this bay, even if it was early morning! 'That's why it's called Sunset Bay,' he said. 'It's sunset here all the time!' Quite enchanted by this, Wendy was keen to look up the bay on Peter's map.

Use your MAP to find which square Sunset Bay is in – then follow the appropriate instruction. If you don't have one, you'll have to guess which instruction to follow.

If you think D4	go to 86
If you think D3	go to 211
If you think E3	go to 41

110

Although Peter didn't have a magic spell book, he soon thought of another way of shifting Wendy. It was quite simple really. Peter merely slid down the inside of the tree himself, jolting Wendy free as he came down on top of her! As they both tumbled out at the bottom of the tree, however, they found that the underground home was empty. The lost boys had disappeared! Searching round for an explanation of their disappearance, Peter discovered a note. 'It's from the pirate, Captain Hook!' he exclaimed with alarm. 'He has taken the last lost boys to his ship as prisoners!' Peter immediately instructed that they fly off in search of this ship! ***Go to 98.***

111

Unfortunately, Peter didn't have his dictionary – but then he suddenly recognised the handwriting on the note! 'It's his . . . the pirate, Captain Hook!' he exclaimed. 'The reason it's so bad is because, ever since I sliced off his right hand, he has had to write with his left!' The children had little interest in this detail, however, and were anxious to know what the note might mean. 'It probably means that Hook has carried them off to his ship!' Peter told them gravely. 'Come – we must fly off in search of it!' Since they would need to fly as fast as possible if the lost boys were to be saved, John gave Wendy, Michael and himself a good sprinkle of fairy dust.

Remove one of the FAIRY DUST CARDS from your TOP-HAT CARD. Now go to 98.

112

The children went to have a closer look at some of the treasure, and Wendy asked Peter who it belonged to. 'A pirate named Captain Hook,' Peter said simply. Wendy gave a little gasp at this, asking if he was a very fearsome pirate. 'Oh yes,' Peter replied quite happily, 'he would make you walk the plank as soon as look at you!' Wendy was so horrified at this that she immediately sprinkled herself and her two brothers with a pouch of fairy dust. Should they suddenly meet Captain Hook, she wanted to be sure that they had enough flying power to escape!

Remove one of the FAIRY DUST CARDS from your TOP-HAT CARD. Now go to 253.

113

Suddenly, Wendy noticed that Tinker Bell's trail of light was twice as bright as usual. She asked Peter what it meant. 'Oh, she always does that when she's excited,' he replied. Wendy wondered the reason for this excitement but then she realised. Of course, Tinker Bell must have just spotted Neverland – because there was the strange island, twinkling away beneath them! They all started to swoop down and came to land at the top of some beautiful, pink-coloured cliffs. John asked Peter if he had a map with him so they could find out which part of the island this was.

Use your MAP to find which square the pink cliffs are in – then follow the appropriate instruction. If you don't have a MAP in your CHARACTER CARD, you'll have to guess which instruction to follow.

If you think B3	go to 32
If you think A3	go to 186
If you think A4	go to 14

114

'*RUMDUM!*' Peter cried when he had found the right magic spell word in his book – and suddenly a piece of string appeared in his hand! He stretched a piece of the sun down so there was something to tie it to and then knotted the string round. 'Five singles to Neverland, please!' Peter ordered when they were all hanging on to the end of the string. The sun happily obliged them, transporting them through the air and then gently dropping them down on one of Neverland's beautiful beaches. ***Go to 103.***

115

It was only then that Peter realised that he didn't have his magic spell book with him! He thought Wendy would insist that they flew to the lost boys' home straight away but she let him have his way. 'All right, Peter, a few adventures first,' she told him, 'but I would like to reach the lost boys' home by nightfall so that I can tuck them up.' John was as excited by the thought of adventures as Peter, and he tossed his hat in the air to show it. He'd forgotten all about the pouches of fairy dust powder, though, and one burst open as the hat hit the ground. Its contents were immediately whisked away by the wind!

Remove one of the FAIRY DUST CARDS from your TOP-HAT CARD. Now go to 208.

116

Before the pirates had the chance to capture any of our heroes, though, there was another blood-curdling cry! Turning round, the pirates saw that they in turn had been surrounded . . . by the redskins! 'The redskins are the sworn enemies of the pirates,' Peter explained to the others. 'They spend their whole lives tracking them down.' The redskins and the pirates now commenced a running battle with each other, all but disappearing into the distance. Wendy suggested that they look through Peter's telescope to find out who was winning.

*Use your **TELESCOPE** to obtain a better view of the battle by placing exactly over the shape below – then follow the instruction. If you don't have one, go to 95 instead.*

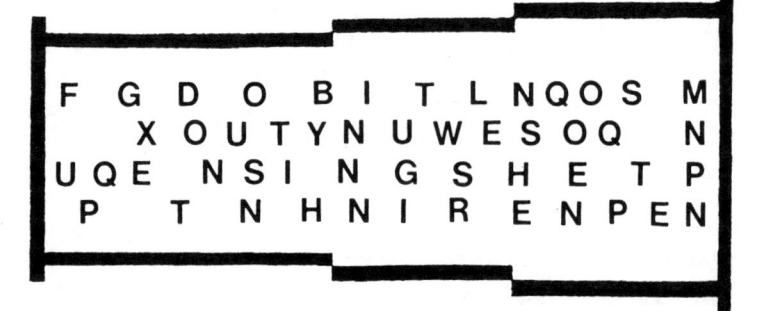

```
F  G  D  O    B  I    T    L  N Q O S    M
     X  O U T Y N  U W E S O Q        N
U Q E    N S I  N  G S H E T       P
   P     T  N  H N I  R   E N P E N
```

117

Learning that Peter didn't have his magic spell book, the children realised that their end was now unavoidable. They were just saying their farewells to each other, however, when it suddenly started to pour with rain. Now the redskins had been praying and dancing for rain for months and so they assumed this must be the work of the children. They immediately untied them and fell prostrate at their feet, as though they were gods. 'Quick, let's fly off before the rain stops!' John said, sprinkling Wendy, Michael and himself with another pouch of fairy dust to make sure they were able to get well away.

Remove one of the FAIRY DUST CARDS from your TOP-HAT CARD. Now go to 18. (Remember: when there are no FAIRY DUST CARDS left in your TOP-HAT CARD the game is over, and you must start again from the beginning.)

118

After an hour or two of flying, Peter at last spotted the home of the lost boys. 'There it is!' he cried, pointing to a group of large trees below them. As they came down to land, he explained that the boys' home was underneath the trees; and that the trees had been hollowed out into separate entrances. 'You just squeeze into the middle of one of the trees . . .' he said, '. . . breathe in so you're thin enough, and you'll slide down!' So they all gathered around one of the trees, preparing to enter . . .

Throw the special DICE to decide who is to enter the tree first.

PETER thrown	go to 151
TINKER BELL thrown	go to 139
WENDY thrown	go to 75
JOHN thrown	go to 10
MICHAEL thrown	go to 55
MAGIC thrown	go to 195

119

As it turned out, the children didn't have to look out for an ice-cream tree because one suddenly sprouted from the ground right in front of them! After they had each plucked their favourite flavour cone from the branches, they continued on their way. Some time later they arrived at the entrance to a huge cave. Peter thought it would be a tremendous adventure to explore inside but Wendy was rather more wary. 'Say there are wolves in there?' she remarked nervously. 'Or maybe even a fiery dragon!' She asked Peter at least to look into the cave through his telescope as a precaution.

Use your TELESCOPE to check if there's anything inside the cave by placing exactly over the shape below – then follow the instruction. If you don't have one, go to 104 instead.

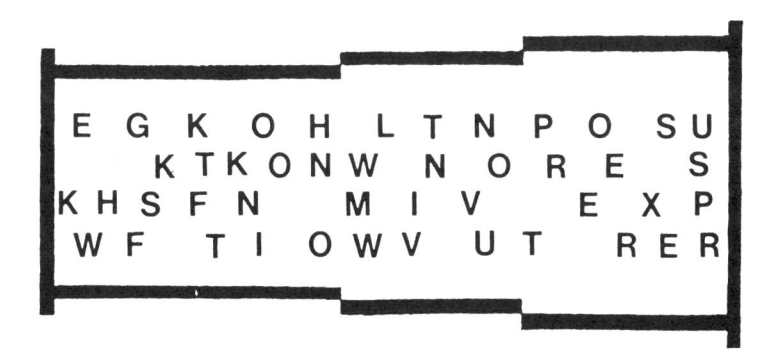

```
E G K O H   L T N   P O   S U
    K T K O N W   N   O R   E    S
K H S F N     M I   V       E  X P
W F   T I   O W V   U T     R E R
```

120

The children now flew down to join the mermaids' hand-bubble game. The teams were mermaid, Wendy and John defending the left goal; and mermaid, Peter and Michael defending the right goal. Tinker Bell was referee, having to tinkle every time the bubble entered one of the goals (which consisted of two rocks sticking out of the water). When the final tinkle came, Wendy was sure her team had won. She made it seven goals to four. But Tinker Bell insisted that Peter's team had won and gave Wendy a fearful warning look in case she dared to dispute the referee's decision! **Go to 40.**

121

'It *is* mother and father!' Wendy cried wistfully, after Peter had lent her his telescope. She saw that their faces were full of panic and concern. 'Perhaps we had better tell them where we're going,'

Wendy suggested guiltily. But just as she prepared to fly down to them, a sudden gust of wind came and blew the children a good way beyond the town. 'That wasn't your doing was it, Peter?' Wendy asked rather suspiciously as she decided she would just have to forget about her parents. Peter had the very faintest twinkle in his eye! ***Go to 196.***

122

'*VIOLET!*' the children all shouted together when Peter had found the right word in his magic spell book. Suddenly, the sun came out from behind a cloud and there was a light shower of rain. And a second or two later, a rainbow appeared, arching right in front of them! 'Just climb on,' Peter said, setting the example, 'and then you'll slide all the way down to that soft patch of grass down there!' ***Go to 197.***

123

Wendy said it was about time Peter took her to the lost boys' home. 'I don't think they should be without their mother for a second longer than necessary,' she remarked. Peter had to confess that he had forgotten where the lost boys' home was, however. 'Perhaps we could ask that funny little creature over there,' John suggested, suddenly spotting a red-capped gnome sitting on a toadstool. So they all went over to the gnome and John doffed his hat. 'Excuse me,' he said in his politest voice, 'but can you tell me where the lost boys' home is?' The gnome gave his reply in Neverlander, though, and so they were going to need a dictionary!

*Use your **NEVERLAND DICTIONARY** to find out what the gnome was saying by translating the instruction in his speech-balloon below. If you don't have one, go to 24 instead.*

DIDDLY PUTT LOD

124

When they had located smugglers' beach on their map, Peter suggested that they explore the caves to see if there were any smugglers still there. 'We could give the dastardly fellows a good fight!' he said, excitedly drawing his sword. John and Michael were so keen to accompany him that Wendy finally agreed to let them go. 'I'll sit on the sand and wait for you,' she told them, '– and mind you don't get any nasty cuts or bruises in the fight!' She needn't have worried, though, because the only thing the boys discovered in the cave was a dictionary!

If you don't already have it there, put the NEVERLAND DICTIONARY CARD into your CHARACTER CARD. Now go to 176.

125

Peter and the children were continuing their journey through Neverland when a flock of Never geese came flying over their heads. Now the Never geese didn't really like Peter very much because he often used to pinch feathers from their wings without asking their permission. So this seemed a perfect opportunity to get a little of their own back! They swooped down, pecking Peter on the head, and one of them whipped John's hat off. 'All our fairy dust pouches are inside!' John cried as the Never goose carried the hat away into the clouds. The children prepared to give chase but the Never goose was now so high up that they could barely see it. A good thing you have your telescope with you, isn't it, Peter!

Does Peter have his TELESCOPE, though? If so, use it to observe the Never goose's flight by placing exactly over the shape below – then follow the instruction. If not, go to 37 instead.

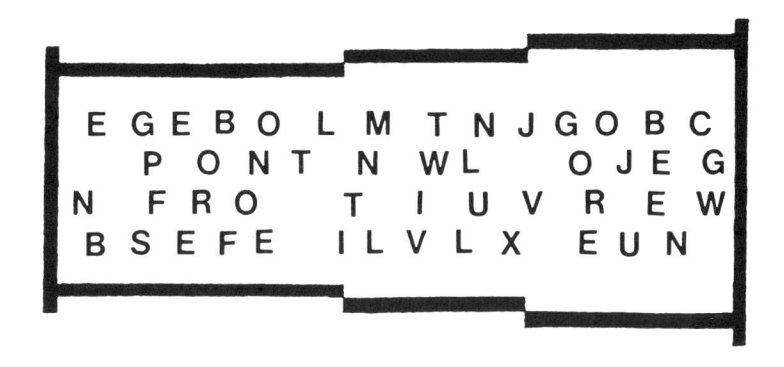

```
E G E B O   L M   T N   J G O B C
    P O N T   N   W L     O J E G
N   F R O     T   I U V   R E W
B S E F E     I L V L X   E U N
```

126
Looking through his telescope, Peter saw that the pirates' ship was moored at the end of the next bay. It wasn't long before the children were being made to board this ship and it set out to sea. 'What filthy decks,' said Wendy as she cast her critical eye over the vessel, 'and look at these grimy port-holes. They look as if they haven't had a good polish for months!' *Go to 158.*

127
'They're telling me to leave their broomstick alone,' Wendy quickly translated the witches' croaks, 'or they'll cast a spell on me!' So Wendy immediately put the broom back where she had found it

and the children hurriedly left the cave. As they were flying along, Wendy asked Peter why the witches had minded so much about her using the broom. After all, she was only doing their cleaning for them! But Peter explained that the witches didn't use brooms for cleaning. They were strictly for flying! ***Go to 84.***

128

'There's an icebag!' Michael suddenly exclaimed after another few minutes. In fact, it was, of course, an ice*berg* but, since he had never seen one before, Michael shouldn't be too criticised! Our adventurers now came down to land on the ice, although it proved a little too slippery for some of them. Not for Tinker Bell, though. She was very graceful and skated around beautifully. Wendy was eager to search for the polar bears as soon as possible but, before she did, she asked Peter to look up this part on his map. It was always a sensible idea to know roughly where you were!

Use your MAP to find which square the iceberg region is in – then follow the appropriate instruction. If you don't have one, you'll have to guess which instruction to follow.

If you think E4	go to 27
If you think D4	go to 8
If you think E3	go to 73

129

When Peter confessed that he had forgotten his magic spell book, the children all shut their eyes, bracing themselves for their fate. But just as the crocodile began licking his lips, deciding which one to start on first, Wendy realised that this didn't have to be their fate after all. They could simply fly away! Of course it was quite understandable that she and her brothers should have forgotten this possibility because they hadn't been flying for very long. But for Peter, who had been able to fly all his life, it really was too much! Anyway, the children quickly took to the air, and John gave Wendy, Michael and himself another sprinkle of fairy dust to make sure they left the crocodile far below!

Remove one of the FAIRY DUST CARDS from your TOP-HAT CARD. Now go to 118. (Remember: when there are no FAIRY DUST CARDS left in your TOP-HAT CARD the game is over, and you must start again.)

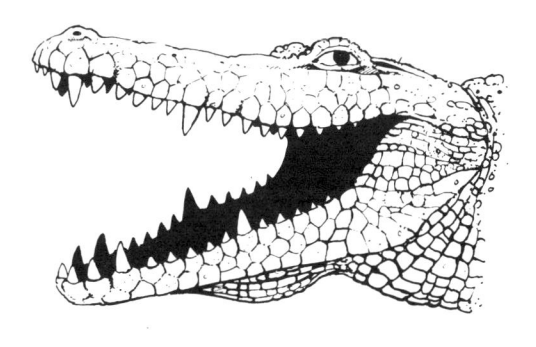

130

Since it would probably take ages to find an igloo *without* a telescope, Wendy decided the best thing to do was just leave. 'But you haven't seen a polar bear yet,' Peter pleaded in that rather spoilt way of his. Wendy was adamant about it though. 'The last thing we want to do is catch cold!' she told him rather sternly. When Wendy, Michael and John tried to take to the air, however, they found that their arms were so numb that they could barely flap them. John had to give them all another sprinkle of fairy dust to help out.

Remove one of the FAIRY DUST CARDS from your TOP-HAT CARD. Now go to 109.

131

With their captain gone, the rest of the pirates – a cowardly lot – immediately surrendered. Peter asked them where the lost boys were, threatening them with the plank if they didn't give a swift answer. Learning that the boys were held on the lower deck, Peter quickly went to fetch them so they could be introduced to their new mother. 'Oh, I do hope they like me!' Wendy said nervously to her two brothers and Tinker Bell as she straightened her dress and tidied her hair. Her fears were completely unfounded, though. For, as soon as the lost boys laid eyes on her, they simultaneously yelled in delight. 'Now, now, boys,' Wendy said with tears welling in her eyes. 'We'll have enough of that din, thank you very much!'

Your adventure has been successful. Well done!

132

They had now been flying for three days and three nights but Neverland was still nowhere in sight. 'Are you sure we're going the right direction, Peter?' Wendy asked a little suspiciously. 'You don't think we might have made the wrong turn at that last horizon?' Peter was highly offended at this, saying that of course they were going the right direction. 'Peter never NEVER loses his way,' he told her boastfully. 'Just keep your eyes open and you should spot Neverland any moment now!'

Throw the special DICE to determine which of them is to spot NEVERLAND first.

PETER thrown	go to 166
TINKER BELL thrown	go to 113
WENDY thrown	go to 279
JOHN thrown	go to 79
MICHAEL thrown	go to 222
MAGIC thrown	go to 232

133

'It's a magic spell book!' Wendy exclaimed when she had used their dictionary to work out the title. She asked Peter who he thought it belonged to. 'Oh, fairies, I expect,' he replied, not sounding half as excited by the discovery as she was. 'They're always leaving their magic spell books around. They're an untidy lot!' Wendy didn't like untidiness either and so she put the magic spell book in her pocket. Besides, it might well come in useful!

If you don't already have it there, put the MAGIC SPELL BOOK CARD into your CHARACTER CARD. Now go to 253.

134

'No, I can't see the lost boys' home anywhere,' Peter said as he pointed his telescope all around. Wendy took the telescope from him, saying she would like a look for herself. 'What does their home look like?' she asked, imagining it to look much like her own home – with walls and a roof and chimneys. 'It's a group of trees,' Peter told her. 'They live underneath them!' Well, Wendy certainly couldn't spot a group of trees anywhere and so it looked as if they would just have to go searching for them after all! ***Go to 208.***

135

Wendy reached the redskin camp first. It would have been Peter but he stopped for a while on the way to have a word with some gnomes he had spotted. Not realising that the redskins were hostile, Wendy landed right in the middle of their camp. (Peter had intended creeping up on them!) She was immediately confronted by the redskin chief, who was covered in war-paint from head to toe. With arms folded, he started speaking to her in a low voice. But he spoke in Neverlander and so Wendy had to wait until Peter came along with his dictionary.

Use your NEVERLANDER DICTIONARY to find out what the redskin chief was saying by translating the instruction in his speech-balloon below. If you don't have one, go to 231 instead.

DIDDLY PUTT
ISH UCK SUL
LOD BLIP

Not long after they had passed Rainbow Bay, Peter said it would be a good time to escape. 'We could fly to the shore while the pirates aren't looking!' he suggested cheekily. 'It's only a short way from here!' Wendy didn't quite share Peter's confidence, though, and worried that they might tire halfway across and be eaten by sharks. 'I'm sure we'd make it if we had another sprinkle of fairy dust,' John chipped in, backing Peter up. So, eventually Wendy was persuaded and, after coating themselves in a whole pouch of fairy dust, they all took off over the ship's side!

Remove one of the FAIRY DUST CARDS from your TOP-HAT CARD. Now go to 18. (Remember: when there are no FAIRY DUST CARDS left in your TOP-HAT CARD, the game is over, and you must start again from the beginning.)

As soon as Peter had uttered the spell word *BROOMSTICK*, the frog changed back to Michael again. He rubbed his eyes with his tiny fists, not sure what had happened to him. The witches were so annoyed that Peter had reversed their spell that they started trying to turn *him* into a frog, and chanted some very horrible words. But Peter called out *BROOMSTICK* again and the witches vanished in a puff of purple smoke! ***Go to 84.***

138

'Ah, there's one!' Wendy exclaimed with delight as she spotted a mermaid through the telescope. It had a beautiful silvery tail and its long hair was also silver – although it looked as if it would probably have been gold in normal light. Wendy became entranced as the mermaid beckoned to her with a long pale finger. 'Stop, Wendy!' John cried as his sister stepped dreamily towards the cliff edge. 'It's trying to lure you to your doom!' Just as Wendy was about to go over the cliff, she noticed a little book at her feet. Fortunately, it broke her trance! 'Look – a magic spell book!' she said as she bent down to pick it up.

If you don't already have it there, put the MAGIC SPELL BOOK CARD into your CHARACTER CARD. Now go to 28.

139

It was decided that Tinker Bell should enter the tree first – her light would make it easier for the rest of them to see. So she fluttered in through a large squirrel-hole in the tree. 'She should be touching the bottom soon,' Peter told the others as he popped his head in the hole, ready for his turn. He was just about to climb in, though, when there was a loud scream from Tinker Bell, which echoed all the way up.

'Something must have happened to her!' Peter cried with concern, and quickly searched under his belt for his telescope.

*Use your **TELESCOPE** to try and see what's happened to Tinker Bell by placing exactly over the shape below – then follow the instruction. If you don't have one, go to 162 instead.*

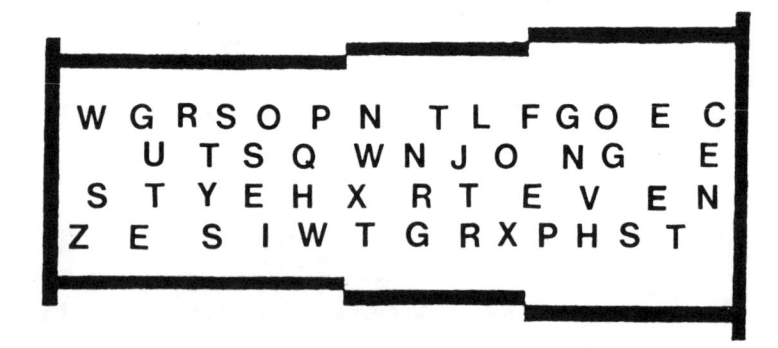

```
W G R S O P   N   T L F G O   E   C
  U T S Q   W N J O   N G       E
S T Y E H X   R T   E V     E N
Z E S I W T   G R X P H S T
```

140

It was just at that moment that Michael sighted Hook's ship, some way to their left. The children immediately flew down towards it, and Peter whipped out his sword ready for battle. 'Hook!' he gave a valiant cry as they alighted on the ship's deck. 'Prepare to meet thy doom!' ***Go to 11.***

141

Peter quickly told Wendy that he didn't have his map, anxious to tell again the story of how he had sliced off Captain Hook's right hand. He was sure it *was* an impressive story! Wendy was determined not to encourage his bragging, though. She didn't feel that slicing off people's right hands was anything to be particularly proud of! 'I'm not listening, Peter,' she told him in a rather bossy, motherly way, 'and I'm afraid that's that!' ***Go to 118.***

142

Despite protests from the others, Wendy finally decided that Michael should fly at the front. That way she could catch on to his ankles if he started to fall! By the time they had left their town way behind, however, Wendy was becoming a little inattentive in her duty. She was so busy watching all the birds fly past that she didn't notice Michael's arms were flapping more and more slowly. Suddenly he began to drop like a stone! 'Oh, quick, Peter – do something!' she cried. Peter told her not to panic: it was just a matter of saying the correct magic spell word from his book and Michael would be saved. But had he remembered to bring the magic spell book with him?

Do you have the MAGIC SPELL BOOK CARD in the slit of your CHARACTER CARD? If so, use it to find the right spell word by placing exactly over the shape below – then follow the appropriate instructions. (Remember to return the MAGIC

***SPELL BOOK** to the **CHARACTER CARD** afterwards.) If you don't have one, you'll have to guess which instruction to follow.*

If you think it's PIXIE	go to 215
If you think it's DWARF	go to 183
If you think it's GIANT	go to 252

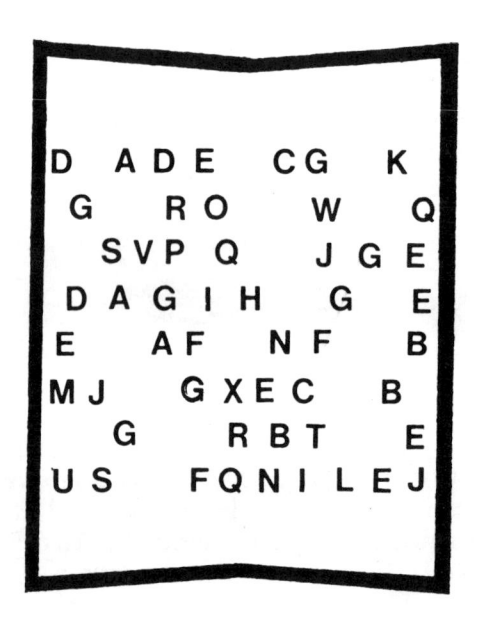

```
D   A D E     C G     K
 G   R O     W       Q
   S V P Q     J G   E
 D A G I H     G     E
E     A F   N F     B
M J     G X E C   B
   G     R B T     E
U S     F Q N I L E J
```

143

When Peter confessed that he had forgotten his map, John had another idea for finding out which part of Neverland they were in. 'I could fly to the top of one of those castle turrets,' he suggested. 'I bet I'd be able to see for miles and miles!' He had flown only about halfway up the castle, however, when he began to run out of flying power. Slowly, he started to drop . . . then faster and faster! He quickly reached under his hat for a pouch of fairy dust and just managed to sprinkle himself with it in time. 'I think I'll forget that idea!' he said bashfully as he returned to the ground.

Remove one of the FAIRY DUST CARDS from your TOP-HAT CARD. Now go to 123.

144

'I bet you left it behind deliberately!' Wendy snapped, when Peter confessed that he had forgotten his Neverland map. She was sure he wanted to find the lost boys only after as many adventures as possible! In fact, she was so annoyed with him that she decided to go straight home and she sprinkled John, Michael and herself with a pouch of fairy dust. Seeing Peter begin to cry, though, her heart softened. 'All right, I'll stay,' she told him gently. 'But I don't want any more adventures than are absolutely necessary!'

Remove one of the FAIRY DUST CARDS from your TOP-HAT CARD. Now go to 208.

145

The pirates captured Peter first, realising that without their leader the others would be helpless. Peter fought and struggled for all he was worth but the pirates at last managed to put him in chains. Despite their noble resistance, John and Michael were soon captured as well which left only Wendy, who did not resist at all. She considered it far too undignified! When they were all firmly bound, Captain Hook came forwards and started to address them. He spoke in Neverlander, though, and so it was a job for their dictionary!

Use your NEVERLAND DICTIONARY to find out what

Captain Hook was saying by translating the instruction in his speech-balloon below. If you don't have one, go to 199 instead.

> DIDDLY PUTT
> LOD ISH

146

No sooner had Peter uttered the magic word *STORM* than the sky was obscured by huge black clouds. A moment later, there was a deluge of rain! The redskins jumped up and down with delight before hurrying off to their wigwams for cover. 'It's all right for them,' grumbled John as the rain dripped from his hat, 'but it's making us soaking wet!' The chief was so grateful to them, though, that he invited them into his wigwam to dry off. He also gave them a Neverland map as a token of peace!

If you don't already have it there, put the MAP into your CHARACTER CARD. Now go to 125.

147

'There's just one fewer than a dozen!' Peter replied gleefully as he counted the redskins through his telescope. So Wendy kept to her word and agreed that the attack should go ahead. When the children had swooped down on the redskins, however, they were in for an unpleasant surprise. There were hundreds of them there! As the redskins quickly overpowered them, Wendy couldn't quite decide whether Peter had deliberately lied about how many there were . . . or whether he just didn't know how to count. She gave him the benefit of the doubt! ***Go to 200.***

148

Michael woke first, stretching out his arms for his mother. But then he remembered that he was in Neverland and that his mother was many hundreds of miles away. He had to admit he was beginning to miss her, but at this particular moment there was something he missed even more – breakfast! Did they have breakfast in Neverland, he began to worry as he quickly wakened the others. Well, it seemed they didn't . . . but Wendy had the good idea of conjuring some up with Peter's spell book!

Use your MAGIC SPELL BOOK to find the right spell word for conjuring up breakfast by placing exactly over the shape below –

then follow the appropriate instruction. If you don't have one, you'll have to guess which instruction to follow.

If you think it's BACON   go to 284
If you think it's MUSHROOM   go to 107
If you think it's KIPPER   go to 246

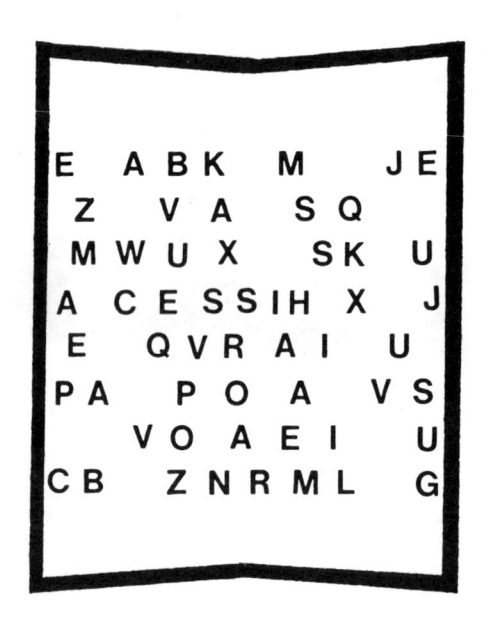

```
E    A B K    M        J E
 Z    V A    S Q
 M W U X      S K        U
A   C E S S I H   X      J
 E    Q V R A I        U
P A    P O   A       V S
      V O   A E I       U
C B    Z N R M L        G
```

149

Looking through his telescope, Peter suddenly spotted a whole field of sticks. They stood upright, growing like wheat! He swooped down to pluck a handful and then brought them back to the children so they could swirl them round in the candyfloss cloud. 'Are you sure the cloud won't mind us tearing off little bits of it, Peter?' Wendy asked, but Peter assured her that the cloud wouldn't mind too much. It was much better than being an ordinary cloud at any rate! Soon after they had finished their candyfloss, Michael spotted the iceberg region ahead and so they all prepared to land. ***Go to 181.***

150

'Oh, how rude!' exclaimed an indignant Wendy as she used Peter's dictionary to translate the mermaid's words. 'She's saying that my hair is far less beautiful than hers!' Peter seemed puzzled by Wendy's indignation. He didn't really know what 'beautiful' meant and he certainly couldn't think that it was anything to become bothered about! Tinker Bell, though, was rather more knowledgeable on the subject; indeed, she giggled gleefully at the mermaid's remark! ***Go to 40.***

151

Peter said *he'd* better enter the tree first himself – to show them how it was done. So he crawled through a squirrel-hole into the very centre of the tree and then drew in his breath. After he had slid down through the tree into the ground, the others took their turn... but when they arrived inside the home they were met with bad news! 'The boys have gone!' said a distraught Peter. 'There's a note here from the pirate, Captain Hook, saying he kidnapped them while they were out playing. He's taken them to his ship as hostages! They've been taken to his ship moored off Mushroom Ring!' Trying to keep calm at this terrible news, Wendy asked Peter to look up Mushroom Ring on his map.

Use your MAP to find which square Mushroom Ring is in – then

follow the appropriate instruction. If you don't have one, you'll have to guess which instruction to follow.

If you think C1	go to 170
If you think C2	go to 212
If you think D1	go to 78

152

'That demon Hook must have put them in irons below!' Peter cursed when he failed to find the lost boys through his telescope. 'Come on, mates, it's time we released them!' And at that Peter led the way down to the pirate ship, landing in the very centre of its deck. 'It's you or me this time, Hook!' Peter addressed his arch-enemy with steel in his voice. 'Draw your sword!' ***Go to 11.***

153

'Ah, just as I thought,' Peter exclaimed as he pointed his telescope in the direction from which the cannonball had come, 'it's Captain Hook!' Wendy anxiously asked to know more about this Captain

Hook and Peter said that he was a pirate who terrorised the seas off Neverland. At that moment, another cannonball came hissing past them and Wendy suggested that they had better land as soon as possible! Not far from where they landed, Michael spotted a little dictionary in the grass. It was a Neverland dictionary – something that could well prove useful!

If you don't already have it there, put the NEVERLAND DICTIONARY CARD into your CHARACTER CARD. Now go to 123.

154

John reached Neverland first; his excitement had given him an extra spurt! 'You only won because I let you!' Peter told him a little sulkily as he arrived a few seconds behind. They found themselves at the top of some high cliffs with waves crashing below. One of the waves suddenly leapt a lot higher than the others, however, drenching them all with spray. 'Where's Tinker Bell?' Peter asked as they all wiped their eyes – but then he suddenly spotted her, dead at his feet! 'The water must have put her light out,' Peter moaned, and began to cry. Wendy kindly patted him on the shoulder, asking if he couldn't magic her better again.

Use your MAGIC SPELL BOOK to find the right magic word to make Tinker Bell better by placing exactly over the shape below –

then follow the instruction. If you don't have one, you'll have to guess which instruction to follow.

If you think it's BUTTERCUP	go to 206
If you think it's ROSEHIP	go to 271
If you think it's FOXGLOVE	go to 57

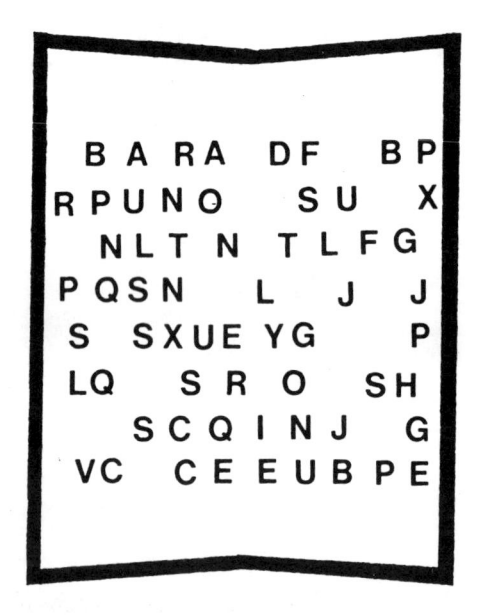

```
B A R A    D F      B P
R P U N O      S U      X
   N L T N   T L F G
P Q S N     L    J    J
 S   S X U E  Y G         P
L Q    S R O      S H
     S C Q I N J      G
 V C    C E  E U B P E
```

155

'There's somewhere nice and soft just down there, over to the right,' Peter said as he scanned the island with his telescope. So they all came to land on a beautiful beach of soft white sand. As John picked himself up, he noticed an old map lying only a metre or so away from him. He handed it to Peter, asking what the skull and crossbones on the front meant. 'It means it belongs to my arch-enemy, Captain Hook!' Peter replied with a strange glint in his eye!

If you don't already have it there, put the MAP into your CHARACTER CARD. Now go to 103.

156

When Peter had found the desert on the map, he suggested playing a game with the vultures. 'What sort of game?' Michael asked with interest and, to illustrate, Peter pretended to collapse on to the sand. Thinking he was dead, the vultures immediately swooped down towards him. But then Peter suddenly jumped up again, frightening them out of their lives! 'Wasn't that fun?' he cried gleefully – but the others were more interested in something they had found in the sand. It was a Neverland dictionary!

If you don't already have it there, put the NEVERLAND DICTIONARY CARD in your CHARACTER CARD. Now go to 61.

157

Following the Never goose's flight through their telescope, the children eventually caught up with it. The Never goose tried to hide behind a little pink cloud but the cloud simply wasn't big enough and its long neck stuck out. Peter not only snatched John's hat back from the goose (fortunately, none of the fairy dust pouches had fallen out!) but he also plucked its largest wing feather as an act of defiance! ***Go to 18.***

158

As the pirate ship set sail, its canvas billowing in the wind, Captain Hook came to gloat at his prisoners. They were then all set to work at various menial jobs on the ship. Peter was put at the wheel to steer, Wendy was ordered to swab the decks, and Michael and Tinker Bell despatched to the kitchens. Poor old John, though, was given the worst job of all because he was made to climb right to the top of the mast as look-out. Sitting petrified in the crow's-nest, he eventually spotted some headstones on the shore. He shouted this information down to Peter at the wheel so he could check their whereabouts on his map.

Use your MAP to find which square the headstones are in – then follow the appropriate instruction. If you don't have one, you'll have to guess which instruction to follow.

If you think A1	go to 5
If you think B1	go to 94
If you think A2	go to 44

159

'The witches are coming back!' Wendy shrieked as she spotted three tiny figures on broomsticks through the telescope. They therefore quickly got their things together, preparing to leave. It was as they were doing this that John spotted a little book on the cave floor. He thought it was probably a book of witches' evil potions and so decided to take it with him to spite them. It was only some time later that he discovered that it was in fact a Neverland dictionary!

If you don't already have it there, put the NEVERLAND DICTIONARY CARD into your CHARACTER CARD. Now go to 38.

160

'It sounds like Tink has spotted a mermaid!' Peter exclaimed as the fairy gave an excited tinkle. So the children searched the water even harder, trying to find the mermaid themselves. 'Oh, come on, Tink – where is she?' Peter implored when they still had no luck. But Tinker Bell was in one of her mischievous moods and refused to help them! 'If you don't tell us,' Peter threatened her, becoming more and more irritable, 'I'll blow all your fairy dust off, and you won't be able to fly!' Wendy thought it was about time she put a stop to the row, and tactfully suggested that Peter use his telescope to help him find the mermaid.

Use your TELESCOPE to try and spot the mermaid by placing exactly over the shape below – then follow the instruction. If you don't have one, go to 241 instead.

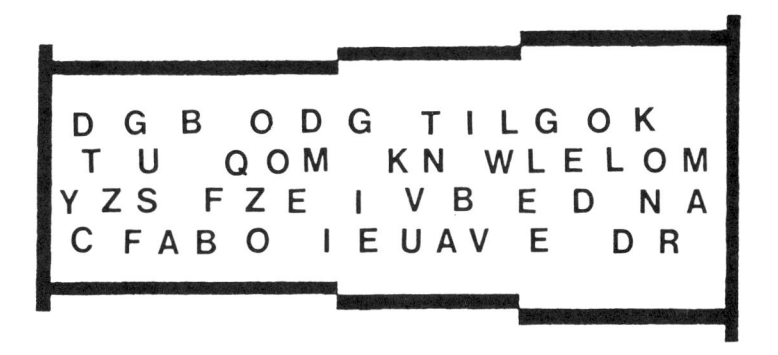

```
D G B   O D G   T I L G O K
 T U   Q O M   K N  W L E L O M
Y Z S  F Z E  I V B  E D  N A
 C F A B  O   I E U A V  E   D R
```

161

'*SNAPPER!*' Peter cried as he at last found the right spell word in his book. It looked as if it had come a fraction too late, though, because Michael had just at that moment dropped between the crocodile's jaws! But a telescope now appeared between these jaws, extending and extending until the crocodile's mouth was wide enough for Michael to crawl out again. He cheekily whipped the telescope out and took it with him as he flew up to rejoin the others!

If you don't already have it there, put the TELESCOPE CARD into your CHARACTER CARD. Now go to 118.

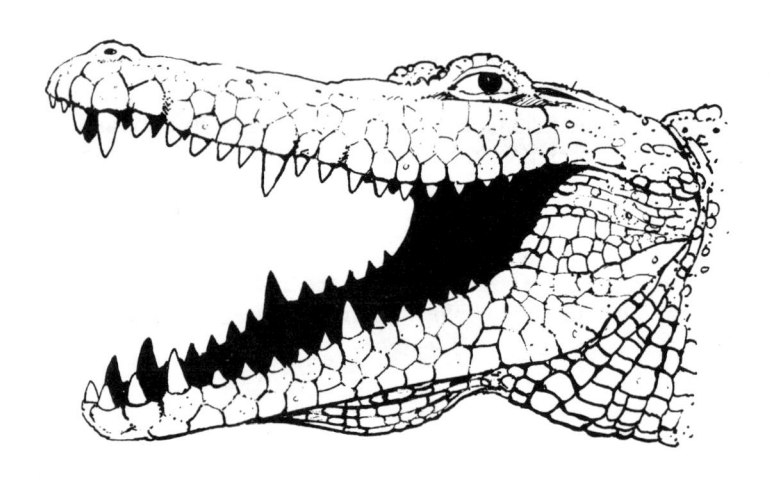

162

Never had Peter more regretted his bad memory. He had forgotten his telescope! There was nothing for it, therefore, but to slide quickly down the tree after Tinker Bell. As Peter reached the bottom, where it emerged into the underground home, he expected to see Tinker Bell badly hurt. But that wasn't the reason for her scream. The reason was that the lost boys were all gone! As he searched round for some explanation for this, he found a note signed by the pirate, Captain Hook. It said that the lost boys had all been captured and taken to Hook's ship as hostages! No sooner had Peter and Tinker Bell rejoined the others above ground than they all prepared to fly off in search of Hook's ship. Since they would need to go as fast as possible, John gave Wendy, Michael and himself a good sprinkle of fairy dust.

Remove a FAIRY DUST CARD from your TOP-HAT CARD. Now go to 98.

163

Checking under his belt, Peter found to his horror that he *had* left the magic spell book behind! 'We'll just have to try *blowing* the cloud away,' John suggested. 'Now when I say the word, all of you give a big puff!' After John had counted 'One-two-three' they all puffed as hard as they could . . . and it worked, the cloud blew right away. The trouble was that the children had used so much energy puffing that they hardly had any left to continue flying. 'We'd better sprinkle ourselves with some more fairy dust,' Wendy said, regretfully taking one of the pouches from under John's hat.

Remove one of the FAIRY DUST CARDS from your TOP-HAT CARD. Now go to 196.

164

Peter was just in the middle of confessing that he didn't have his map when Hook's ship suddenly sailed into view ahead of them! 'Follow me, lads!' Peter cried, so full of excitement that he momentarily forgot they weren't all lads in his company. He swooped down on to the *Jolly Roger*'s deck, whipping out his sword as he spotted Hook. 'It's you or me this time, blackguard!' he told him, and they immediately set at each other's steel. John was so spellbound by this terrifying duel that at one point he stood a bit too close and Hook's sword sliced off the top of his hat. One of the fairy dust pouches started to leak all over his hair!

Remove a FAIRY DUST CARD from your TOP-HAT CARD. Now go to 11. (Remember: when there are no FAIRY DUST CARDS left in your TOP-HAT CARD the game is over, and you must start again.)

165

When Peter looked under his belt for his Neverland dictionary, however, he found that he had forgotten it. 'Well, can't you speak Neverlander without a dictionary?' John asked with surprise. Peter said of course he could – at least, he had been able to but he had forgotten that as well! Tinker Bell at last finished her stream of abuse and, after one final glare at Wendy, continued flying. She deliberately went a lot faster this time, though, and the only way the children could keep up was by sharing a pouch of fairy dust between them.

Remove one of the FAIRY DUST CARDS from your TOP-HAT CARD. Now go to 196.

166
'There it is, down there!' Peter cried out suddenly. 'See, I told you we'd be there soon – and I *knew* I would spot it first!' He now led the way down to that strange-looking land, the others following excitedly. They all came down with a gentle bump on some cliffs at the island's extreme corner. Right next to where they landed was a large sign with some strange words on it. 'Is it in Latin?' John asked, having just started to study Latin at school. Wendy told him not to be so silly, though. It was in Neverlander, of course – and she asked Peter if he had a Neverland dictionary with him so she could work out what it said.

Use your NEVERLAND DICTIONARY to find out what the

sign said by translating the instruction below. If you don't have one in your CHARACTER CARD, go to 100 instead.

167

While Peter and Wendy were searching for Treasure Beach on the map, John went to have a closer look at one of the treasure chests. Tucked amongst all the gold and silver, he found a long brass telescope! 'Who's Captain Hook?' he asked Peter, noticing the name engraved down the telescope's side. Peter gasped, his eyes doubling in size. 'Captain Hook is my dreaded enemy!' he told them. The children all looked at each other in dismay. They only hoped that they didn't make the acquaintance of this Captain Hook!

If you don't already have it there, put the TELESCOPE CARD into your CHARACTER CARD. Now go to 253.

168

'I've spotted you, Tink!' Peter warned the mischievous fairy as he pointed the telescope up into the leaves. He then gave the ice-cream tree a good shake to try and make her fall out. 'Oh, I'm sure it was just an accident, Peter,' Wendy said with concern, but it was too late – Tinker Bell suddenly crashed down to the hard ground! Peter immediately began to cry, thinking he had killed her, but then he too received an ice-cream cone slap in the face. Tinker Bell was suddenly up in the tree again, as naughty as before! ***Go to 61.***

169

The children were still looking out for the icebergs when a pink, sticky cloud came floating towards them. 'It's a candyfloss cloud,' Peter said as if it didn't really need any explanation. 'They're clouds that become fed up with just being grey and ordinary.' The boys asked eagerly if they could eat some of the cloud as it passed. 'Of course,' replied Peter, as if this was a silly question, 'but you'll need sticks to twirl the candyfloss on.' He said he would search for some down below through his telescope.

Use your TELESCOPE to try and spot some sticks by placing exactly over the shape below – then follow the instruction. If you don't have one, go to 76 instead.

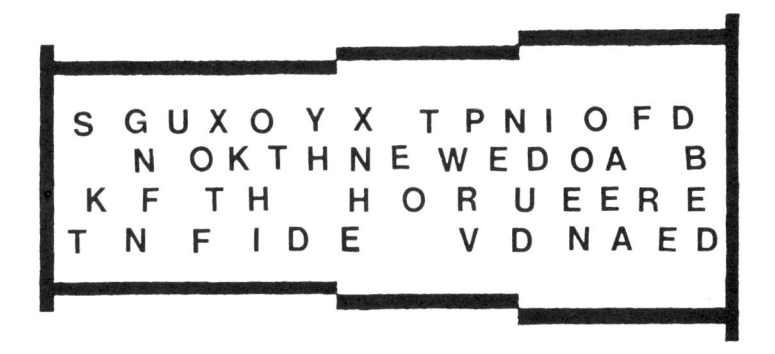

```
S  G U X O  Y X   T P N I  O F D
   N  O K T H N E  W E D  O A     B
K  F   T H     H  O R  U E E R   E
T  N  F  I  D E      V  D  N A E D
```

170

Having located Mushroom Ring on his map, Peter said they must go there in search of Captain Hook's ship at once. As they were preparing to climb back up the tree to the outside, however, Wendy couldn't help noticing how messy the lost boys' home was. Socks and shirts were scattered all over the floor and the bed had been made with great big lumps in it! Since this really wouldn't do, she decided to give it a quick tidy before leaving. It was as she was tidying that she found, under a pile of pyjamas, a Neverland dictionary!

If you don't already have it there, put the NEVERLAND DICTIONARY CARD into your CHARACTER CARD. Now go to 98.

171

'Let's build ourselves an ice-house instead!' Peter suggested enthusiastically, after he had admitted that he didn't have his magic spell book. So they all started to cut big blocks out of the ice, stacking them on top of each other like bricks. At last the ice-house was completed and they all crawled through the little hole they had left as a door. 'We'll call this a Wendy ice-house!' said Peter as their hands and feet soon started to warm up again. ***Go to 109.***

172

Unfortunately, Peter *didn't* have his magic spell book – and so it looked as if they would have to walk the plank after all! The pirates chose John to go first, forcing him nearer and nearer the end of the plank with little prods of their swords. One final prod . . . and John was plummeting to the water below! But he didn't reach it because he suddenly remembered he could fly and flapped his way back on to the deck. The pirates couldn't understand what had gone wrong, and made him walk the plank again. But again he merely flew back! This happened a third time, and a fourth – and, eventually, the pirates just gave up the idea of making them all walk the plank. All those trips had wasted so much of John's flying power, however, that he needed another good sprinkle of fairy dust!

Remove one of the FAIRY DUST CARDS from your TOP-HAT CARD. Now go to 36.

173

Wendy reached Neverland first. She won the race not because she was the fastest flier but because she was the one who was most eager to see Neverland. 'Oh, isn't it beautiful!' she exclaimed as she sat in the overgrown grass. The grass was not green-coloured as she was used to . . . well, some of it was, but some of it was orange and purple and blue! As she was running her hand through the blades of grass, wishing that it was like this at home, she suddenly found a little book. The title on the front was in Neverlander, however, and so it would need a Neverland dictionary to work out what it said.

Use your NEVERLAND DICTIONARY to find out the title of the book by translating the instruction below. If you don't have one, go to 90 instead.

DIDDLY
PUTT
LIG UCK
SUL
ONG DINK

174

Just as Peter was looking for his magic spell book, there was an almighty flash of lightning. 'We don't need a rainbow after all,' Peter said delightedly. 'We could slide down one of those instead!' Wendy wasn't so sure, though. The forks of lightning looked awfully scary and dangerous! But Peter eventually persuaded her so they all waited for the very next stroke of lightning and quickly made a grab for it. Just in case they fell off halfway down, John sprinkled them all with a pouch of fairy dust so they would have enough flying power. It was a good thing he did because the lightning burnt their hands so much that they were soon forced to let go!

Remove one of the FAIRY DUST CARDS from your TOP-HAT CARD. Now go to 197.

175

Wendy had completely forgotten that Peter didn't have a map! 'Well, never mind,' she said. 'Let's just fly out of here as quickly as possible because I don't really like it. It looks the sort of place that would have snakes wriggling along the ground!' But when Wendy, John and Michael tried to take off, they found that their toes hardly left the ground. 'It looks as if we need another sprinkle of fairy dust,' John said. 'I'll get a pouch from under my hat!'

Remove one of the FAIRY DUST CARDS from your TOP-HAT CARD. Now go to 61.

176

Wendy, John and Michael were just showing Peter how to build sand-castles on the beach when there was a blood-curdling cry from behind them. Turning round, they saw a band of fierce-looking men carrying sabres. 'It's Captain Hook and his pirates!' Peter exclaimed. 'We're surrounded!' The children tried to make their escape but the pirates closed in on them to take them captive . . .

Throw the special DICE to decide which of the children the pirates capture first.

PETER thrown	go to 145
TINKER BELL thrown	go to 225
WENDY thrown	go to 25
JOHN thrown	go to 244
MICHAEL thrown	go to 82
MAGIC thrown	go to 116

177

'I don't have my magic spell book!' Peter glumly confessed to Wendy. The pirates now made the children walk towards their ship, *Jolly Roger*, which was moored just around the corner. 'It looks as if we're being press-ganged,' John whispered anxiously. Peter said it might be even worse than that, though. They might be made to walk the plank! *Go to 158.*

178

They had flown only halfway to the redskin camp when one of the puffs of smoke sailed towards them and swallowed them up! It then carried them back to the redskin camp, dumping them at the chief's feet. Wendy, John and Michael gave a big gulp as he bent down to speak to them. He spoke in Neverlander, though, and so they would need a dictionary to find out what he was saying. Was he telling them that they were to be scalped, perhaps . . . or tied to a totem pole and left to perish in the sun!

*Use your **NEVERLAND DICTIONARY** to find out exactly what the chief had in store for them by translating the instruction in his speech-balloon below. If you don't have one, go to 105 instead.*

DIDDLY PUTT BLIP

179

Since Peter didn't have a telescope, Wendy decided they had better leave the cave as quickly as possible. But first Peter wanted to play a trick on the witches. 'Oh, do hurry up, Peter,' Wendy urged him as he started to change some of the ingredients in the witches' evil potion book, 'they could be back soon!' Peter was just altering *four frogs* to *seven conkers* in the book's wart-growing recipe when Michael spotted the witches flying towards them. They were all in such a hurry to leave the cave that John forgot to pick up one of his pouches of fairy dust!

Remove one of the FAIRY DUST CARDS from your TOP-HAT CARD. Now go to 38.

180

'Oh, how can we help her when we don't know what she's saying?' Wendy said frustratedly when Peter admitted that he didn't have his magic spell book. But Peter told her that the mermaid didn't want help. 'She's not crying because she's unhappy,' he explained, 'but because her tears make the sea deeper. They don't like it when it's too shallow in case they bump their heads when they dive.' Wendy now realised why the sea always had a salty taste! It was now time for the children to be off and so John sprinkled Wendy, Michael and himself with another pouch of fairy dust. He'd noticed the flapping of their arms had got a bit weak lately!

Remove a FAIRY DUST CARD from your TOP-HAT CARD. Now go to 28.

The children had flown a good few miles from the iceberg region when Wendy spotted a huge crocodile in the mud below. 'I once fed that crocodile a hand,' Peter told the others boastfully. 'It was the right hand of Captain Hook, the pirate. I sliced it off in a duel!' Peter couldn't remember whether he had already told the children this story but he was so proud of it that he didn't think it would suffer from repetition! Just as they were passing over the crocodile, Michael got cramp in his arms and started to fall. Wendy quickly asked Peter to look up a magic spell book to save him!

Use your MAGIC SPELL BOOK to find the right spell word for saving Michael by placing exactly over the shape below – then follow the appropriate instruction. If you don't have one, you'll have to guess which instruction to follow.

If you think it's SNOUT	go to 65
If you think it's CROCK	go to 97
If you think it's SNAPPER	go to 161

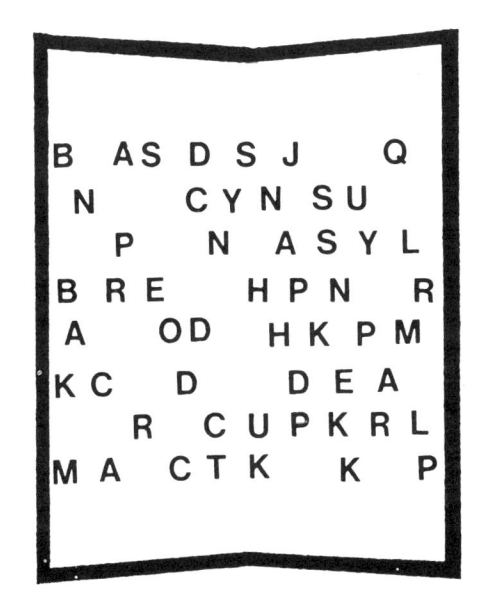

```
B   A S   D S   J       Q
 N       C Y N   S U
    P     N   A S Y L
B  R E       H P N       R
A     O D     H K P M
K C     D       D E A
     R   C U P K R L
M  A   C T K     K     P
```

182

'*BEANPOLE!*' Peter called down the inside of the tree when he had found the right word in his magic spell book. Wendy suddenly became quite a few centimetres thinner and, as a result, started to move again. It wasn't all good news, though, because when she reached the bottom of the tree she found the underground home was empty. 'The lost boys have disappeared!' she told the others with concern when they finally joined her. Looking round for a clue to their disappearance, Peter suddenly discovered a telescope. 'It belongs to Captain Hook, the pirate!' he exclaimed breathlessly. 'He must have taken the lost boys away to his ship. Quick, we must go and find it!'

If you don't already have it there, put the TELESCOPE CARD into your CHARACTER CARD. Now go to 98.

183

I hardly dare relate this – but, no, Peter hadn't remembered to bring his magic spell book with him! 'Well, there must be something you can do!' Wendy pleaded with him, tears in her eyes. Peter scratched his head. 'I could swoop down and catch him, I suppose,' he replied slowly and thoughtfully. He took a deep breath like a diver and plunged into the night below. Just before Michael hit the ground, Peter darted underneath him, heaving him up on his back. 'I don't know what all the fuss was about!' he said casually as he returned Michael to the others. ***Go to 132.***

'There's a mermaid!' John exclaimed with delight. The mermaid pulled herself up on a rock and was soon joined by several others. The children now flew down to meet them but Peter was surprised to find that their reception for him wasn't as friendly as it normally was. It seemed that they didn't like Wendy's golden hair – no, not one little bit – for it almost rivalled their own! They soon dealt with that, though, by casting a spell which turned it green! 'Oh!' Wendy cried as she caught a reflection of it in the water. 'Quick, Peter, tell me a magic spell so I can change it back again!'

Use your MAGIC SPELL BOOK to find the right spell word for this by placing exactly over the shape below – then follow the appropriate instruction. If you don't have one, you'll have to guess which instruction to follow.

If you think it's MISCHIEF	go to 64
If you think it's NAUGHTY	go to 275
If you think it's IMPISH	go to 108

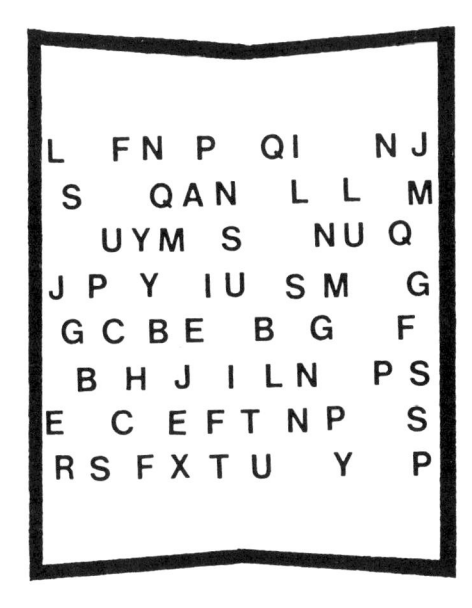

```
L  F N  P  Q I      N J
 S   Q A N   L L    M
   U Y M  S    N U  Q
J P  Y   I U  S M    G
 G C B E   B G      F
   B H J  I L N   P S
E  C  E F T N P    S
R S F X T U    Y   P
```

185

'It looks as if I have left my magic spell book behind,' Peter confessed to the others when he had checked under his belt and found that it wasn't there. 'Never mind,' he added jauntily, 'you can all wait here while I fly back to fetch it.' Wendy told him he would do no such thing, though – he couldn't just leave them there unprotected. It was then that John had a brilliant idea. If they all jumped up and down, it might make the cloud rain . . . and, as everyone knows, if a cloud rains hard enough, it will eventually disappear. The idea worked a treat. The cloud had soon dissolved into thousands of tiny raindrops and the children were able to continue on their way. ***Go to 196.***

186

Checking under his belt, Peter replied that he didn't have a map. 'Well, how do we know where we are in Neverland?' John asked but Peter didn't really seem that bothered. He was eagerly preparing for his adventures, practising his sword-play. He was so intent on it that he accidentally knocked John's hat off. John quickly grabbed for the pouches of fairy dust as they fell out but one dropped over the edge of the cliff. They all watched in desperation as it burst open on the sharp rocks below!

Remove one of the FAIRY DUST CARDS from your TOP-HAT CARD. Now go to 197.

187

Peter spotted an ice-cream tree first. Of course, he had the advantage that he was the only one there who knew what they looked like. Although, to be fair, the ice-cream tree looked exactly as you would expect it to look – with little cornets sprouting from the branches! They all picked and ate three cornets each and it was a good thing they did so, because they soon arrived at a vast desert. There was nothing there but giant cacti, and the odd vulture circling in the sky. Wendy asked Peter to look up the desert on his map so they would know where they were.

Use your MAP to find which square the desert is in – then follow the appropriate instruction. If you don't have one, you'll have to guess which instruction to follow.

If you think A3	go to 175
If you think B4	go to 243
If you think B3	go to 156

188

Peter and the boys were becoming very restless to attack the redskins and so Wendy finally agreed that they could. 'Don't come running to me if they scalp you, though!' she warned, wagging her finger. To begin with, the children's attack went very well; the redskins were completely taken by surprise. But as soon as the redskins got to their bows and arrows, the tide of the battle changed. 'I think we'd better surrender,' Wendy said as the arrows came whistling past their ears. In fact, one arrow even penetrated John's top-hat, and pierced one of the fairy dust pouches in the process!

Remove one of the FAIRY DUST CARDS from your TOP-HAT CARD. Now go to 200.

189

'So who's winning?' the boys asked Wendy excitedly as she watched the battle through the telescope. Wendy quietly folded up the telescope and returned it to Peter. 'I'm afraid the pirates have won,' she informed them despondently, 'and now they're heading straight back for us!' They couldn't decide whether they should stand and fight, or flee. As a result they didn't really do either, allowing themselves to be captured. The children were now forced aboard the pirates' ship and taken out to sea! *Go to 36.*

190

John woke first, thinking he was in his nursery for a moment, but then he remembered that it was a cave. As the others began to wake up (some – notably Tinker Bell – more lazily than others), John noticed a large cauldron in the corner. There were also some horrible dead frogs and snakes and things there. 'This looks like a witches' cave,' he said anxiously. 'They must have been out for the night on their broomsticks. They'll probably be returning soon!' Worried that the witches might put a curse on them all if they were discovered in the cave, Wendy asked Peter if she could borrow his telescope. She wanted to keep a close watch on the sky for them!

Use your TELESCOPE to see if there's any sign of the witches' return by placing exactly over the shape below – then follow the instruction. If you don't have one, go to 179 instead.

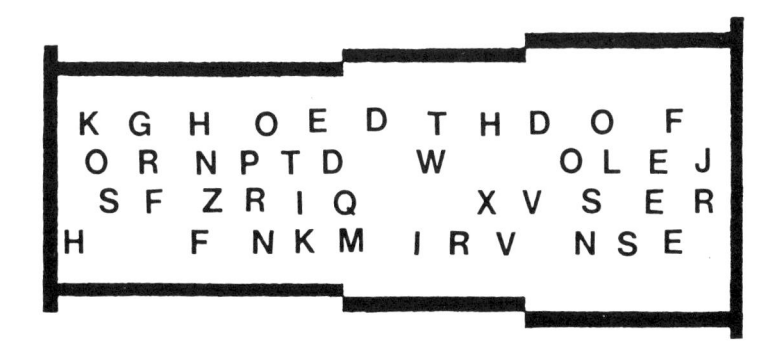

```
K  G   H  O  E   D   T  H  D   O     F
O  R   N  P  T   D   W        O  L  E  J
 S  F   Z  R  I  Q         X  V   S  E  R
H      F   N  K  M   I  R  V    N  S  E
```

191

'I don't have a telescope, Wendy,' Peter told her when he had checked under his belt. 'Now, let's fly away from here before it's too late!' It looked as if it *was* too late, though, because John was already stepping dreamily towards the cliff edge! The wailing sound had completely entranced him! One more step and he was over . . .

tumbling towards the sharp rocks at the cliff bottom! Fortunately, one of his pouches of fairy dust came open as he tumbled, completely coating the inside of his hat, and he just managed to fly up again in time!

Remove one of the FAIRY DUST CARDS from your TOP-HAT CARD. Now go to 28.

192

'There's a rather nice little igloo just over there,' said Wendy, pointing to her right, as she looked through Peter's telescope. They all made the quick flight towards it and then crawled through the little hole that was its entrance. 'Ah, a little untidy – but it will do!' approved Wendy as they made themselves comfortable. She was giving the place a quick clean – snapping off any icicles that had grown too long – when she discovered a Neverland dictionary on the floor. Since there was no bookshelf for it and it only seemed to mess the place up, she decided that they should take it with them.

If you don't already have it there, put the NEVERLAND DICTIONARY CARD into your CHARACTER CARD. Now go to 109.

193
Peter moved his telescope all around but the lost boys were still nowhere to be seen. It seemed that the lost boys were indeed *lost*! When he returned underground to the others, however, he learnt the reason for this. 'I've found this note signed by Captain Hook, the pirate!' a distraught Wendy told him. 'He says that he has kidnapped the boys and taken them aboard his ship as hostages!' Although knowing full well that this was a trap set for him, Peter immediately ordered that they fly off in search of Hook's pirate ship! ***Go to 98.***

194
As they were looking out over Rainbow Bay, Wendy noticed one of the pirates shyly smiling at her. He wore little round glasses and didn't look half as fearful as the other pirates, so Wendy smiled back. This emboldened him and he coyly came forward to introduce himself. 'My name's Smee, ma'am,' he said, performing an awkward bow. He then handed her a shiny brass telescope as a token of his humble admiration.

If you don't already have it there, put the TELESCOPE CARD into your CHARACTER CARD. Now go to 77.

The children were still deciding who should enter the tree first when Wendy noticed that it was behaving rather strangely. Its branches were shaking – even though there wasn't so much as a breath of wind about! Then its leaves started to fall . . . but autumn was long since past! 'What's the matter, tree?' Wendy asked gently, realising that the falling leaves were tears and that it must be upset. Between sniffs, the tree gave its reply – but it was in Neverlander and therefore a job for Peter's dictionary!

Use your NEVERLAND DICTIONARY to find out what the tree was saying by translating the instruction in its speech-balloon below. If you don't have one, go to 213 instead.

196

'How much further do we have to go?' little Michael asked when they had been flying for two whole nights and two whole days. Peter said Neverland should be just beyond the next couple of horizons and so they all kept their eyes peeled. Suddenly, a hazy island appeared way, way below, bathed in a golden light. 'That's it,' Peter said simply. 'Let's race down and see who reaches it first!'

Throw the special DICE to determine who wins this race.

PETER thrown	go to 242
TINKER BELL thrown	go to 69
WENDY thrown	go to 173
JOHN thrown	go to 154
MICHAEL thrown	go to 46
MAGIC thrown	go to 264

197

Their landing over, they now prepared to explore the island. Peter explained that he had to re-explore Neverland every time he returned to it. This was partly because he was very forgetful and partly because . . . well, exploring was much more fun anyway. 'You mean to say that you don't remember where the lost boys are exactly?' Wendy asked with reproach, having very little time for carelessness. When Peter replied that this was so, Wendy suggested that he might at least try and save a bit of time by looking through his telescope.

*Use your **TELESCOPE** to try and spot the lost boys by placing exactly over the shape below – then follow the instruction. If you don't have one, go to 33 instead.*

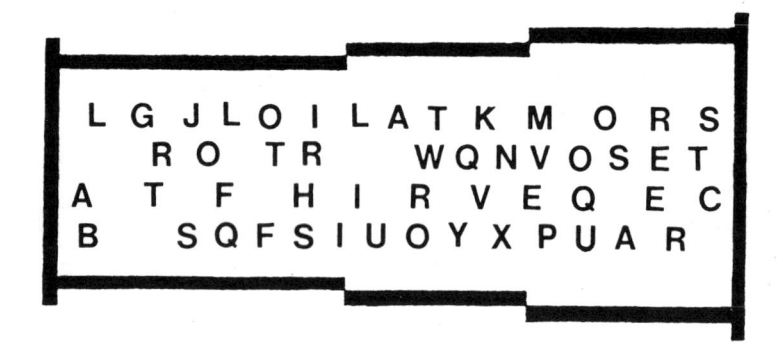

```
L G J L O I L A T K M   O R S
    R O   T R       W Q N V O S E T
A   T F   H I   R V E Q   E C
B     S Q F S I U O Y X P U A R
```

198

Embarrassed to admit that he had forgotten his magic spell book, Peter pretended that he didn't mind one of the other flavours after all. Besides, he had more important things to worry about – his shadow had suddenly run away! It was so offended at being left on the ground while Peter had gone up into the ice-cream tree that it decided to make a break for it. Peter desperately flew after it, with the others following close behind. Finally, the shadow was caught again but the children were so tired after the chase that they had to give themselves another good sprinkling of fairy dust.

*Remove one of the **FAIRY DUST CARDS** from your **TOP-HAT CARD**. Now go to 61.*

199

Although Peter didn't have his dictionary, he said he could quite easily guess what Captain Hook was saying. He was telling them that they were to be taken aboard his ship as prisoners! And so it proved – for all the children were pushed towards a little rowing-boat and then taken out to the waiting *Jolly Roger*. John tried to buy their freedom by offering one of the pirates a pouch of fairy dust. But the blackguard double-crossed him and so they were one pouch short for nothing!

Remove a FAIRY DUST CARD from your TOP-HAT CARD. Now go to 158.

200

The redskins tied the children to a totem pole and began to do a war dance around them. 'These war dances usually last about an hour or so . . .' Peter explained as they struggled in vain against the ropes, '. . . then we'll be sacrificed!' The Darling children couldn't believe how calm Peter was about it all but then they supposed he must just be used to danger. The hour was nearly up when Wendy suddenly had an idea. Peter could look up a spell in his magic spell book to whisk them far away from there!

Use your MAGIC SPELL BOOK to find what the right spell

word is by placing exactly over the shape below – then follow the appropriate instruction. If you don't have one, you'll have to guess which instruction to follow.

If you think it's MOCCASIN	go to 117
If you think it's TOMAHAWK	go to 226
If you think it's WIGWAM	go to 26

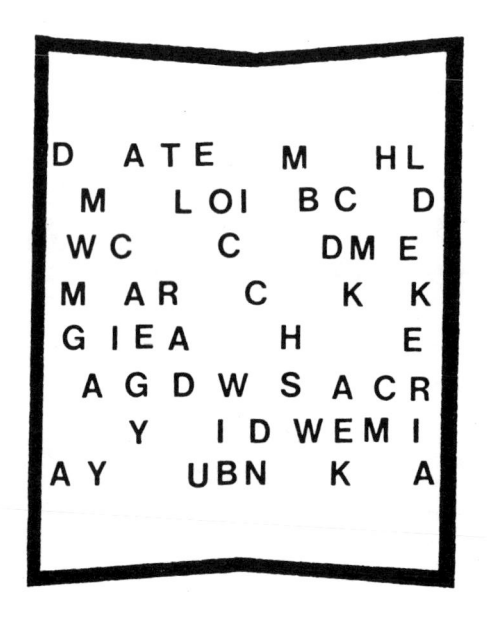

```
D   A T E     M     H L
  M   L O I   B C   D
 W C    C       D M E
 M   A R   C     K   K
 G   I E A     H     E
  A G D W   S   A C R
      Y   I D W E M I
A Y     U B N   K   A
```

201

Since Peter didn't have his magic spell book, he drew out his sword, intending to force the witches to change Michael back again. But the witches quickly mounted their broomsticks and fled into the sky. 'Oh, what do we do now?' cried Wendy as Michael gave a pathetic little croak . . . but then John suddenly had an idea. 'It might not work at all,' he said cautiously, 'but we could try sprinkling Michael with a pouch of fairy dust and see if that changes him back. We'll either have Michael back with us again or a flying frog!' Fortunately, it was the former – Michael suddenly changed back to his usual toddler self!

Remove a FAIRY DUST CARD from your TOP-HAT CARD. Now go to 84.

202

Unfortunately, Peter didn't have his magic spell book – but he did have an idea instead! 'Tinker Bell's light becomes warmer the more she flies about,' he said. 'So I'll make her fly around in little circles between us all and we can warm our hands by her!' To the others this seemed rather cruel but Tinker Bell didn't want their sympathy. She would do anything for Peter! In fact, the idea worked very well and their hands became warmer and warmer as Tinker Bell flapped and flitted for all she was worth. But her wings eventually became so tired that they could no longer support her in the air. John had to sprinkle one of his pouches of fairy dust over them to restore their strength.

Remove one of the FAIRY DUST CARDS from your TOP-HAT CARD. Now go to 109.

203

Peter and the children were still trying to spot the waterfall when they were enveloped by a tornado! They were completely powerless as it swirled them round and round. But it must have been a friendly tornado because, when it finally released them, the children found themselves above the sea. And there, right beneath them, was Hook's ship! 'I'll use my telescope to see if the lost boys are on deck,' said Peter, reaching under his belt.

Use your TELESCOPE to try and spot the lost boys by placing exactly over the shape below – then follow the instruction. If you don't have one, go to 88 instead.

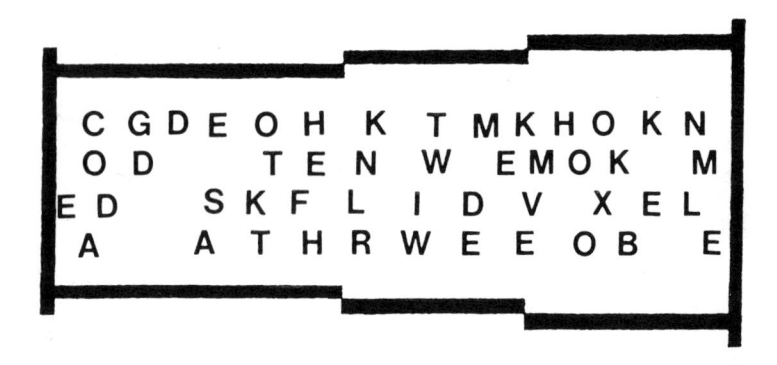

```
C G D E   O H   K   T M K H O   K N
O D       T E N   W   E M O K     M
E D     S K F L   I D V   X E L
A       A T H R W E E   O B       E
```

204

Without his magic spell book, Peter did not know which magic spell word was appropriate! Anyway, it hardly mattered because he soon spotted Neverland, shimmering in the distance. He led the flight down to one of its beautiful beaches but John was so eager that he flew rather more upside down than he should have done. Suddenly, off came his top hat! 'Quick, the fairy dust pouches!' he cried as they fell out. Unfortunately, they were unable to retrieve one of the pouches, but it could have been a lot worse!

Remove one of the FAIRY DUST CARDS from your TOP-HAT CARD. Now go to 103.

205

It was at last agreed that John should fly at the front. Peter wasn't too happy about this to begin with – he was always used to being the leader himself – but Wendy promised to tell him a story on the way in return. They had been flying for a good hour or so when John felt an itch on his head. He lifted his top-hat to scratch it but completely forgot that the pouches of fairy dust were there and they all fell out! The children desperately squinted at the ground below, trying to spot where they had landed. 'I'll see if I brought my telescope with me,' Peter said with sudden inspiration, checking under his belt.

Do you have the TELESCOPE CARD in the slit of your CHARACTER CARD? If so, use it to see if you can spot the pouches of fairy dust by placing exactly over the shape below – then follow the instruction. (Remember to return the TELESCOPE to the CHARACTER CARD afterwards.) If you don't have one, go to 45 instead.

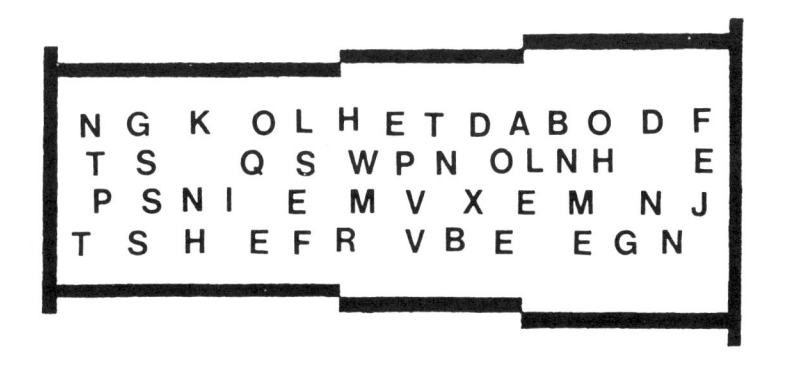

```
N G  K  O L H E T D A B O  D  F
T S     Q S W P N O L N H     E
P S N I  E M V X E M  N J
T S H  E F R  V B E   E G N
```

206

'*BUTTERCUP!*' Peter said rather quietly after he had flicked through his magic spell book for the right word. He had never tried this spell before and so he didn't know whether it would work.

Slowly, Tinker Bell's light came on again, though, and it was soon as bright and sparkling as before! 'Of course, I wasn't really crying,' Peter boasted, now that his friend was perfectly all right again. 'It was just some of that sea-spray in my eyes!' ***Go to 123.***

207

'No, you mustn't take any of the treasure,' Wendy shouted to John and Michael as she suddenly noticed them stuffing some of the gold pieces into their pockets. 'That would be stealing!' she added. Peter gave a loud chuckle at this, telling her that the treasure was *there* to be stolen. 'It belongs to Captain Hook, you see,' he explained. 'And if we steal it, that gives him an excuse to fight us!' Wendy pretended to understand . . . but in truth she thought this the strangest place she had ever been! ***Go to 253.***

208

They had been exploring Neverland for a good couple of hours now but the lost boys' home seemed as far away as ever. 'I hope they all remember to brush their teeth before they go to bed,' Wendy said, worried that they might not reach them now until tomorrow. John and Michael had worries of a very different nature – they had yet to see any food in Neverland! 'I'm hungry,' moaned Michael, rubbing his tummy. Peter asked if they would all like an ice-cream. 'Well, look out for an ice-cream tree, then,' he said when the children had eagerly replied that they would. 'There are plenty of them in Neverland!'

Throw the special DICE to decide who is to spot an ice-cream tree first.

PETER thrown	go to 187
TINKER BELL thrown	go to 272
WENDY thrown	go to 4
JOHN thrown	go to 49
MICHAEL thrown	go to 93
MAGIC thrown	go to 119

209

'*SPYGLASS!*' Peter cried out in a firm, clear voice and suddenly something very strange happened to the ship's plank. It started to grow in length! It grew to five metres long, then ten, then twenty. Soon it had reached fifty metres and was still on the increase. Well, of course, it would now take the children so long to walk the plank that it would ruin all the pirates' fun. So they rather sulkily decided to let the children off! *Go to 36.*

210

Peter and the children were still trying to spot a mermaid when something very strange started to happen down in the cove. A sort of eerie grey descended over it, just as if it were dark, and then a quiet wailing sound began. It echoed from rock to rock. 'We must fly away from here at once,' Peter told the others tensely. 'That's the sound of the mermaids trying to lure us off the cliffs!' Wendy was still anxious to obtain a glimpse of a mermaid, though, and so begged Peter for a quick look through his telescope before they left.

Use your TELESCOPE to try and spot a mermaid by placing exactly over the shape below – then follow the instruction. If you don't have one, go to 191 instead.

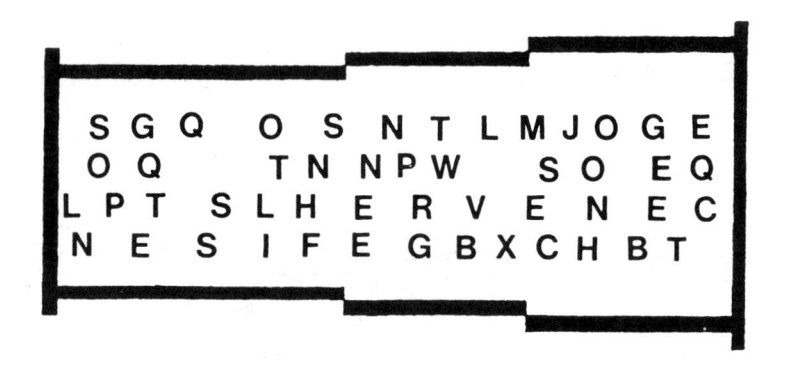

```
S G Q    O S   N T L M J O G   E
O Q      T N  N P W    S O    E Q
L P T  S L H  E R V   E  N   E C
N  E  S  I F E  G B X C H  B T
```

211

At that very moment a big green snout broke through the surface of the water! Then the snout opened and two rows of razor-sharp teeth appeared. 'There's a crocodile down in the bay!' Wendy, John and Michael shrieked in unison. Peter told them it was nothing to be afraid of, though – the only person who need be afraid of it was the pirate, Captain Hook! 'When I cut Hook's right hand off in a duel,' he explained casually, 'I threw it to the crocodile for his supper. The crocodile liked it so much that now it spends all its time searching for the rest of him!' The children were still a little doubtful about the crocodile's appetite, though, and so John quickly sprinkled them all with a pouch of fairy dust to make sure they didn't suddenly drop down into its jaws!

Remove one of the FAIRY DUST CARDS from your TOP-HAT CARD. Now go to 118. (Remember: when there are no FAIRY DUST CARDS left in your TOP-HAT CARD the game is over, and you must start again from the beginning.)

212

The children quickly climbed up the hollow tree to the outside again. They were just about to fly off in search of Captain Hook's ship when John noticed that one of his pouches of fairy dust was missing. 'It must have fallen out while we were down below,' he said. He wanted to return underground to look for the missing pouch but Peter said there wasn't time, and so he just had to leave without it.

Remove one of the FAIRY DUST CARDS from your TOP-HAT CARD. Now go to 98.

213

Although Peter didn't have a dictionary , he soon discovered the reason for the tree's misery. For, pinned to its bark was a note signed by the pirate, Captain Hook! It said that he had attacked the lost boys' home and taken them away to his ship as prisoners. Peter angrily screwed the note up and threw it to the ground, immediately ordering that they prepare to fly off after Captain Hook's ship. Since he wanted to make sure they didn't flag on the way, John sprinkled his sister, brother and himself with another pouch of fairy dust!

Remove a FAIRY DUST CARD from your TOP-HAT CARD. Now go to 98.

214

Even though they didn't have a map with them the children soon managed to find Wailing Lake, and came to land on its shore. The breezes had seemed almost to guide them there, as if they too were concerned for Tiger Lily's fate. She was bound hand and foot on a rock in the middle of the lake . . . and the evil water was already lapping at her waist. Peter immediately prepared to dive in to rescue her but Tinker Bell pulled him back by the hair. She didn't want him risking his life for some silly female! Since the seconds were running out, John therefore decided to go in his place. He just managed to free Tiger Lily in time but his hat floated off in the water and one of the pouches became so wet that the fairy dust lost all its power!

Remove one of the FAIRY DUST CARDS from your TOP-HAT CARD. Now go to 125.

215

'*PIXIE!*' Peter called out quickly (it was fortunate that he *did* have the magic spell book with him, tucked under his belt), and Michael's descent immediately came to a halt. '*PIXIE!*' Peter uttered the magic spell word again and this time Michael started to rise. He rose and rose until he was at their level once more. 'No wonder you had such trouble flying, Michael,' Wendy said, spotting a large Neverland dictionary tucked under his pyjamas. She asked him where he had found it. Michael replied that it had just been lying around on their bedroom floor. 'It sounds as if some silly, forgetful person dropped it there,' Wendy remarked, giving Peter a meaningful look.

If you don't already have it there, put the NEVERLAND DICTIONARY CARD into the slit of your CHARACTER CARD. Now go to 132.

216

Suddenly, Peter had one of his rather mischievous ideas. 'Let's fly all the rum barrels to the top of that cliff up there so the smugglers can't find them!' he suggested gleefully. So he, John and Michael made several short flights to the cliff-top and back, carrying a barrel on each trip. At last the work was over but John and Michael had used up so much flying power that now they could barely leave the ground. They had to sprinkle a whole pouch of fairy dust on themselves before they acquired the art again!

Remove one of the FAIRY DUST CARDS from your TOP-HAT CARD. Now go to 176.

217

Peter reached the redskin camp first, quietly coming to land behind a rock. The others arrived soon after, crouching down at Peter's side. 'Are they peaceful redskins or hostile redskins?' Wendy asked in a whisper. She kept her fingers crossed, hoping Peter would say peaceful; but, *'Hostile!'* he replied cheerfully. John then suggested looking up the redskin camp on the map so they would know where they were.

Use your MAP to find which square the redskin camp is in – then follow the appropriate instruction. If you don't have one, you'll have to guess which instruction to follow.

If you think C3	go to 30
If you think C2	go to 188
If you think B2	go to 267

218

At that very moment, though, the witches returned, filling the cave's entrance with their hideous silhouettes! 'Quick, flee, before they put a curse on us and turn us into frogs!' Peter cried. So the children immediately took to the air and made a break for the outside. The witches mounted their broomsticks, hot in pursuit. They drew nearer and nearer – almost in spell-casting range – and so John quickly sprinkled a pouch of fairy dust over Wendy, Michael and himself to try and help them fly a bit faster. 'We've done it!' cried John with relief when the witches gave up at last.

Remove one of the FAIRY DUST CARDS from your TOP-HAT CARD. Now go to 84.

219

Wendy spotted the icebergs first, pointing over to her right. They now came down to land on the ice but it was so cold that the children started to shiver. And, as for Tinker Bell, her tinkle had a decidedly creaky sound to it! 'If only we had brought some nice warm clothes with us!' sighed Wendy; then she suddenly had an idea. Maybe Peter could conjure some up with his magic spell book!

Use your MAGIC SPELL BOOK to find the right magic word for conjuring up some warm clothes by placing exactly over the

shape below – then follow the appropriate instruction. If you don't have one, you'll have to guess which instruction to follow.

If you think it's SHIVER	go to 171
If you think it's TREMBLE	go to 228
If you think it's SHUDDER	go to 202

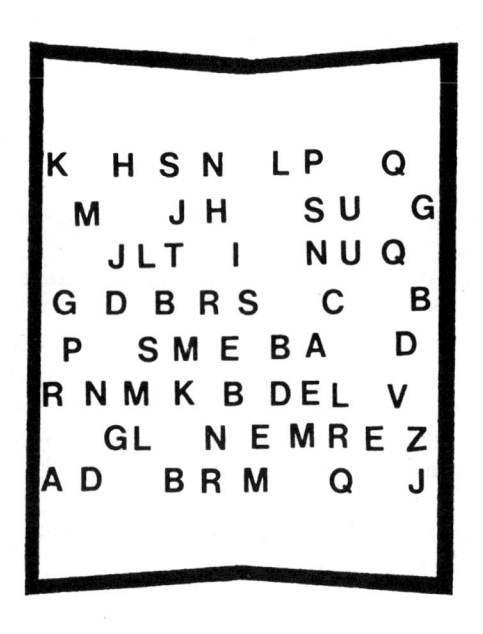

```
K  H S N   L P     Q
  M   J H     S U    G
    J L T  I   N U Q
 G D B R S    C      B
 P   S M E B A       D
 R N M K B D E L     V
    G L   N E M R E  Z
 A D    B R M     Q  J
```

220

'Peter, are you sure you can't remember just a tiny bit of Neverlander?' Wendy pleaded when he told her that he didn't have his dictionary. Peter insisted that he couldn't, though, and so there was no way they could make sense of the Never bird's directions. Fortunately it didn't matter because a few seconds later they were just able to detect a fearsome singing in the air. It was Captain Hook's pirates! Following the abominable sound, they soon found themselves hovering directly above Hook's ship. 'Hook, draw your sword!' Peter cried at his arch-enemy after he had led the swoop down. The children watched the terrible duel and John threw his hat in the air to spur Peter on. He'd completely forgotten that the fairy dust pouches were inside, however, and one dropped out, splitting open on the deck!

Remove a FAIRY DUST CARD from your TOP-HAT CARD. Now go to 11.

221

'I've forgotten my magic spell book,' Peter confessed, 'but it doesn't matter because I know of another way to make it rain. We just puff and puff until a cloud comes and then we fly up and give it a pinch so that it starts to cry!' Although this seemed a little cruel, the others agreed to the idea and began puffing. No sooner had the cloud appeared than they flew up to pinch it. The cloud immediately burst into tears, showering everywhere with rain! As they were returning from this successful mission, however, Wendy suddenly felt her arms weaken. John quickly sprinkled her with a pouch of fairy dust before she began to fall!

Remove a FAIRY DUST CARD from your TOP-HAT CARD. Now go to 125.

222

'There it is!' Michael shouted when he spotted a beautiful, shimmering island in the distance. Although Michael had never been to Neverland before, he knew exactly what it would be like. For he had often imagined it in his dreams! Peter and Tinker Bell did an absolutely perfect landing on Neverland but the three Darling children came down with a bit of a bump. You must remember that although they were quite used to flying by now, this was the first landing they had ever made. As Wendy rubbed the slight bruise on her knee, she heard Tinker Bell laugh something at her in Neverlander. Certain that it wasn't very complimentary, she asked Peter for his Neverland dictionary so she could translate!

Use your NEVERLAND DICTIONARY CARD to find out what Tinker Bell is saying by translating the instruction in her speech-balloon below. If you don't have one, go to 280 instead.

DIDDLY PUTT ONG KER

223

'It *is* Captain Hook!' Peter shouted delightedly as he peered through his telescope, 'there's the Jolly Roger!' Michael asked what the Jolly Roger was and Wendy patiently explained that it was the flag flown by pirates. Then she suddenly realised what she was saying! 'Pirates!' she exclaimed with horror. 'Oh, Peter, you don't mean to say that your friend Captain Hook is a pirate?' Peter confirmed that he was – although he said Hook wasn't his friend, he was his arch-enemy! Wendy was just about to ask more when John noticed a map at his feet. It was a map of Neverland – and the most exquisitely-drawn map he had ever seen!

If you don't already have it there, put the MAP into your CHARACTER CARD. Now go to 253.

224

Discovering that Peter didn't have his magic spell book, Wendy quickly thought about how else she could pacify him. 'Can't you just make-believe one of the ice-creams is chocolate-flavoured?' she asked. Now Wendy didn't really have much hope for this suggestion but there was nothing Peter liked more than make-believe. In fact, he often make-believed entire meals – even if there wasn't a single morsel in sight! 'Good idea! Why didn't I think of that?' he exclaimed as he gave one of the ice-creams a joyful lick. ***Go to 61.***

The pirates captured Tinker Bell first, one of them roughly plucking her out of the air with his hairy fist. They knew that with Tinker Bell as a hostage, Peter wouldn't dare resist. Tinker Bell tinkled for all she was worth, probably telling Peter not to bother about her, and flee while there was still a chance, but Peter immediately laid down his sword and surrendered. The others were soon captured too, and manacles were hastily snapped on to their wrists. 'Peter,' Wendy whispered to him, 'couldn't you use your magic spell book to magic us out of this?'

Use your MAGIC SPELL BOOK to find the right spell word for this by placing exactly over the shape below – then follow the appropriate instruction. If you don't have one, you'll have to guess which instruction to follow.

If you think it's KEELHAUL	go to 71
If you think it's CROSSBONES	go to 177
If you think it's TATTOO	go to 17

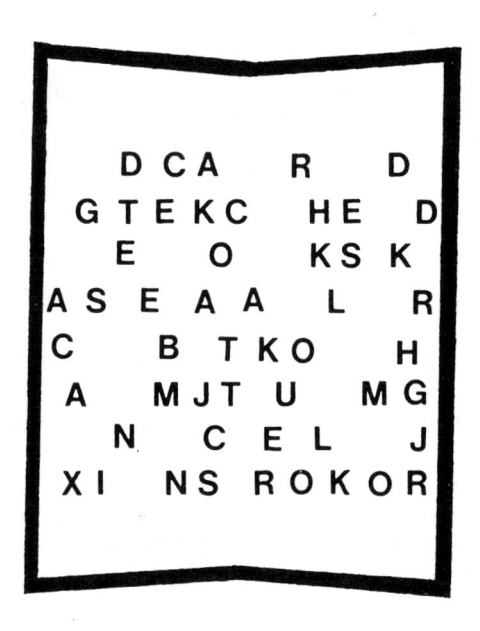

```
      D C A     R      D
   G T E K C   H E    D
     E   O     K S K
 A S   E A A     L      R
 C     B   T K O        H
   A   M J T   U     M G
     N   C   E L        J
 X I   N S   R O K O R
```

226

When Peter told Wendy that he didn't have his magic spell book, they decided there was nothing they could do but resign themselves to their fate. Peter and the children had completely forgotten about Tinker Bell, however. Tinker Bell was so small that the redskins hadn't seen her and she had spent the last half hour pulling and tugging at the children's bonds. At last she managed to free them all (although she had been more than a little tempted to leave Wendy's knots!) and the children quietly flew up into the air. To make sure Wendy, Michael and himself were able to climb well out of the range of the redskins' arrows, John gave them another sprinkle of fairy dust.

Remove one of the FAIRY DUST CARDS from your TOP-HAT CARD. Now go to 18. (Remember: when there are no FAIRY DUST CARDS left in the your TOP-HAT CARD the game is over, and you must start again from the beginning.)

227

Although Peter didn't have his dictionary, he was sure he could guess what the witches were croaking. 'They don't like you using their broom,' he explained to Wendy. 'You see, it's not for sweeping but for flying on!' So Wendy quickly handed the broom back to the witches but, when they sat on it and tried to make it fly, it wouldn't budge! 'You must have spoilt all its magic!' Peter told Wendy accusingly. 'They'll probably cast a spell on us now and turn us all into frogs!' Fortunately, John had a sudden brainwave which saved them from this fate. He sprinkled the witches' broom with a pouch of fairy dust and it immediately lifted from the ground!

Remove one of the FAIRY DUST CARDS from your TOP-HAT CARD. Now go to 84.

228

'*TREMBLE!*' Peter read out the spell word from his book – and, suddenly, they all found themselves clad in nice warm furs! Peter and the boys had brown bear furs while Wendy had a polar bear fur. She felt white was rather more becoming! Not to be outdone,

Tinker Bell had a blue bear fur. I'm not so sure there *are* blue bears but such things are of little hindrance to a fairy's vanity! **Go to 109.**

229

Peter spotted the waterfall first himself, pointing out its tumbling steam below. It wasn't much longer now before they arrived at the sea and they scanned its blue horizons for a ship. 'There she is!' Peter cried and he immediately prepared to lead the swoop down on it. Wendy halted him, though, suggesting he check how many pirates were on deck first. They didn't want to be too outnumbered! 'Just count them through your telescope, Peter,' she told him.

Use your TELESCOPE to obtain a clearer view of the pirates by placing exactly over the shape below – then follow the instruction. If you don't have one, go to 239 instead.

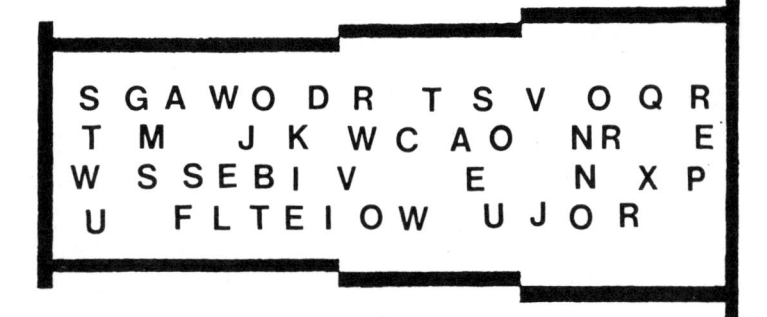

```
S G A W O  D R  T S V   O Q  R
T M   J K W C A O   N R     E
W  S S E B I V     E    N X P
U   F L T E I O W   U J O R
```

230

Just as Wendy had located the whirlpool on the map, Peter gave a joyful cry. 'There's Captain Hook's ship – straight ahead!' he exclaimed, and he immediately led the flight down. As soon as the children had alighted on the *Jolly Roger*, Peter demanded to see the pirates' captain. 'Draw your sword, Hook!' Peter commanded as the handsome demon emerged from his cabin. 'Your time has come!' ***Go to 11.***

231

When Peter did eventually arrive, though, it was only to inform Wendy that he didn't have his dictionary. But Peter wasn't really that interested in what the redskin chief was saying anyway. There was only one thing redskins were good for – and that was fighting! So Peter immediately drew his sword and Tinker Bell and the boys rallied to his side. But the odds were far too much against them and, when John received a flaming arrow through his hat, it seemed time to surrender. Unfortunately, the arrow set fire to one of the fairy dust pouches and the contents exploded in a beautiful puff of golden smoke!

Remove one of the FAIRY DUST CARDS from your TOP-HAT CARD. Now go to 200.

232

They were still trying to spot Neverland when the sun started to act rather strangely and began floating towards them. 'It's pretending to be a balloon,' Peter explained as the ball of gold drifted this way and that. 'It sometimes gets bored being in the same position all the time.' He then had an idea. If they could tie a piece of string to the sun, they could all hang on to it and ask it to float them to Neverland. Where would they find some string, though? 'Couldn't you magic some by saying one of your magic spell words?' Michael suggested.

Use your MAGIC SPELL BOOK to find the right magic spell word by placing exactly over the shape below – then follow the instruction. If you don't have one you'll have to guess which instruction to follow.

If you think it's FLOBTOB	go to 47
If you think it's RUMDUM	go to 114
If you think it's CLOPCLIP	go to 204

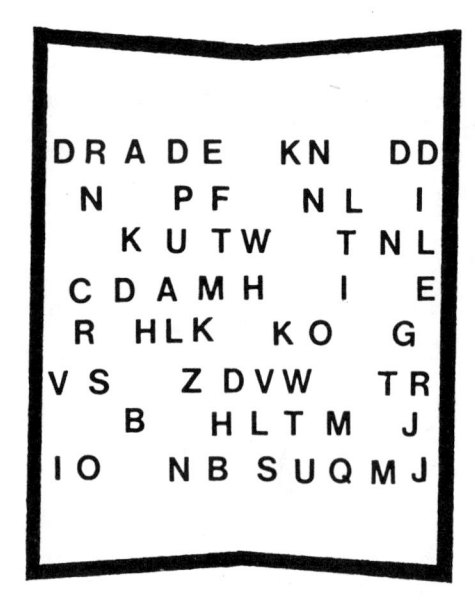

```
D R A D E   K N   D D
 N   P F   N L   I
   K U T W   T N L
 C D A M H   I   E
 R  H L K   K O   G
V S   Z D V W   T R
   B   H L T M   J
 I O   N B S U Q M J
```

233

The children managed to find Wailing Lake without a map because the wails suddenly emanated from it loud and clear. 'That must mean Tiger Lily doesn't have much time!' Peter said as they all flew in the direction of the eerie sound. He was right because, when they arrived there, the evil water was already lapping at the beautiful redskin's waist. A few more seconds and they would have been too late! Peter immediately dived into the water and untied Tiger Lily's bonds so she could swim to safety. 'What a wicked, ungallant creature that Captain Hook must be!' Wendy remarked. Peter gave a quiet, solemn nod! ***Go to 125.***

234

As they were looking out over Rainbow Bay, it suddenly occurred to the children that the shore wasn't too far away. In fact, it was probably near enough to fly to! So, when the pirates were all turned the other way, they leapt over the ship's side. About halfway to the shore, however, Wendy suddenly felt herself begin to lose height. Her feet dropped nearer and nearer to the sea! Fortunately, John just had enough time to sprinkle her with some more fairy dust before it was too late.

Remove one of the FAIRY DUST CARDS from your TOP-HAT CARD. Now go to 18. (Remember: when there are no FAIRY DUST CARDS left in your TOP-HAT CARD the game is over, and you must start again from the beginning.)

235

As soon as they had located the witches' cavern on their map, Wendy suggested that they leave before the witches returned. 'If they find that we have been sleeping in their cave, they might put a curse on us,' she remarked anxiously. They were just about to fly off when John discovered a magic spell book at his feet. Flicking through the pages, he saw that it contained all sorts of horrible spells. There were spells for making warts grow on people's noses, spells for changing little boys into frogs and spells for changing frogs into little boys. He decided to steal it so that the witches couldn't do any more wickedness!

If you don't already have it there, put the MAGIC SPELL BOOK CARD into the CHARACTER CARD. Now go to 84.

236

Peter was the first to spot the icebergs himself, doing a little somersault in the air as he did so. 'See! I told you there were cold parts in Neverland,' he said cockily. But Wendy wasn't so sure coming here was such a good idea after all. They had left their bedroom back at No. 14 so quickly that they were dressed only in their pyjamas – really not at all warm enough for this sort of weather! As she was starting to shiver, she insisted that they find somewhere to shelter. She asked Peter if he had his telescope so she could scan the horizon for an igloo.

Use your TELESCOPE to try and spot an igloo by placing exactly over the shape below – then follow the instruction. If you don't have one, go to 130 instead.

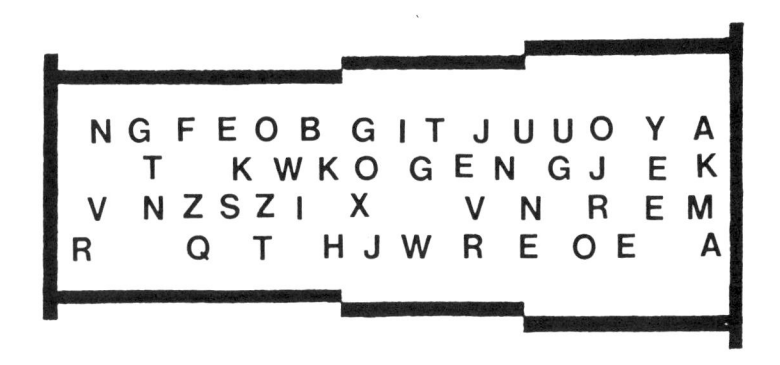

```
N G F E O B  G I T  J U U O  Y A
   T   K W K O  G E N  G J   E K
V  N Z S Z I  X       V  N   R E M
R    Q  T   H J W  R  E  O E    A
```

237

'Oh, Peter,' Wendy tutted at him a little crossly, when she had located Mermaid Cove on his map, 'this place is absolutely *miles* out of the way from the lost boys' home!' But her rebuke was wasted because Peter had already leapt off the cliffs and flown down to join the mermaids' game. He showed them a few tricks they could do with the bubble; like bouncing it off one's head and putting a spin on it so it deceived the opponent. The mermaids were so grateful for this coaching that they gave him a magic spell book as a present!

If you don't already have it there, put the MAGIC SPELL BOOK CARD into your CHARACTER CARD. Now go to 40.

238

'There doesn't *seem* anything wrong with her,' Peter told the others as he pointed his telescope down the hollow of the tree. He expected to see Tinker Bell's frail little body wounded, the light draining out of her. But there she stood, the light as bright and sparkling as usual. 'It must be something she found down there,' Peter said, preparing to slide down the tree himself to investigate, but Tinker Bell came up instead. In her hand was a note! 'It's from the pirate, Captain Hook!' Peter said gravely as he read it. 'He's kidnapped the lost boys and taken them to his ship. We must go and rescue them!' ***Go to 98.***

239

Peter didn't like to admit that he had forgotten his telescope, so he just pretended that he didn't care how many pirates there were on deck! 'The more, the merrier!' he cried as he led the swoop down to the ship. No sooner had Peter landed than he drew his sword, fencing his way through the pirates until he stood face to face with Hook. 'Prepare to meet thy doom!' Peter cried at him and an almighty duel began. At one point the tip of Peter's sword snapped off, flying towards John's hat. Unfortunately, it pierced one of the fairy dust pouches inside!

Remove a FAIRY DUST CARD from your TOP-HAT CARD. Now go to 11. (Remember: when there are no FAIRY DUST CARDS left in your TOP-HAT CARD the game is over, and you must start again from the beginning.)

240

'We should be coming to the sea at any moment now,' Peter told Wendy as he found the waterfall on his map. It was shown only about half a mile away. Sure enough, the sea soon appeared beneath and there, crashing through the waves, was Captain Hook's ship! With a gallant cry, Peter led the way down, alighting nimbly on the ship's deck. 'Hook!' he addressed his arch-enemy, brandishing his sword, 'prepare to meet thy doom!' ***Go to 11.***

241

'I don't *have* my telescope!' Peter told Wendy bad-temperedly. 'Now, come on, Tink, this is your last chance. *Where* is the mermaid?' Tinker Bell seemed to realise that she couldn't push her luck any further and flew down towards the water. A moment or so later there was a high-pitched scream as she pulled the mermaid's hair. '*There's* the mermaid!' exclaimed Peter, turning towards the scream. As he leant forward to have a look, John suddenly lost his hat over the cliff edge. Fortunately, the wind blew it back to him but not before one of the fairy dust pouches had fallen out!

Remove one of the FAIRY DUST CARDS from your TOP-HAT CARD. Now go to 40.

242

Peter reached Neverland first, landing with a cocky little roll. 'I knew I'd win!' he shouted gleefully as he jumped back on to his feet. They found themselves on a large sandy beach, littered with treasure chests. The children had never seen so much gold and silver but Peter seemed quite nonchalant about it, saying there was plenty of treasure on Neverland. 'What's this beach called?' Wendy asked, and Peter replied, 'Treasure Beach, of course!' Wendy then asked him if he had his map with him so they could look up exactly where they were in Neverland.

Use your MAP to find which square Treasure Beach is in – then follow the appropriate instruction. If you don't have one, you'll have to guess which instruction to follow.

If you think B4	go to 112
If you think A3	go to 167
If you think A4	go to 207

243

But Wendy had forgotten that Peter had forgotten the map! 'I suppose that makes us just as bad as each other,' she said. The desert was becoming much too hot for comfort and so they decided to fly off immediately. But it was even hotter up in the sky than it was down below and the children felt their arms growing heavier and heavier. 'If we begin to drop, those greedy-looking vultures are sure to have us!' John said with alarm. Wendy therefore suggested another sprinkle of fairy dust each to revitalise them.

Remove one of the FAIRY DUST CARDS from your TOP-HAT CARD. Now go to 61.

The pirates captured John first . . . then Michael, Wendy, and Tinker Bell. Peter managed to put up a gallant resistance but the odds were against him and he too was finally put in irons. The children were then made to board the pirates' ship. After the ship had sailed out to sea, the anchor was dropped. 'They'll make us walk the plank,' Peter whispered. The children were terrified at this but Peter said they could cast a magic spell to escape. 'But are you sure you've got your magic spell book, Peter?' asked Wendy.

Use your MAGIC SPELL BOOK to find the right magic word to escape by placing exactly over the shape below – then follow the appropriate instruction. If you don't have one, you'll have to guess which instruction to follow.

If you think it's CROW'S-NEST   go to 172
If you think it's PORTHOLE   go to 273
If you think it's SPYGLASS   go to 209

```
M  K C H   E R     P
 F   B OA  A W   D
   I L S R Q   S U T
   N G  P B    H   C
 B   E  Y  O     J
   S G  R L R  A P L
    S    M  E V S R
 X Y   U T A   L S B
```

245

'Oh, what are we going to do?' cried Wendy, when Peter told her that he didn't have his magic spell book. 'Couldn't Michael just stay as a frog?' Peter suggested simply, failing to understand why she was making such a fuss about it. But then he saw tears well in Wendy's eyes and he sprang into action. He whipped out his sword and pinned the three witches against the cave wall. 'Turn the frog into the boy again or you're doomed!' he ordered in a terrifying voice. Shaking from the top of their conical hats to their toes, the witches obeyed him immediately. Although he looked a little confused, Michael suddenly became his old self again! ***Go to 84.***

246

Peter confessed that he didn't have his magic spell book . . . but added that it didn't matter because he could go out hunting for breakfast. So Wendy and the others built a nice big fire while they waited for Peter's return. 'Perhaps he'll bring us back some ostrich eggs,' said Wendy, 'and I do hope he remembers some milk!' But Peter didn't really like these sensible sorts of things for breakfast. They were the things parents made you eat and, not having parents, Peter was rather spoilt. If I tell you that he returned from his hunting trip with an armful of toffee-apples, you'll know exactly what I mean! ***Go to 38.***

247

'Look – down there!' exclaimed Peter, suddenly spotting a mermaid himself. 'There are two of them playing hand-bubble in the water!' The mermaids were bare down to the waist and had beautiful gleaming tails of blue and silver. Their long golden hair tossed about as they patted the rainbow-coloured bubble from one to the other. Peter was all for joining in their game but Wendy insisted that he wait a moment until she had found Mermaid Cove on his map. She wanted to make sure they hadn't come too far out of their way.

Use your MAP to find which square Mermaid Cove is in – then follow the appropriate instruction. If you don't have one, you'll have to guess which instruction to follow.

    If you think C4   go to 120
    If you think D4   go to 237
    If you think E4   go to 257

248

'Perhaps the penguins are asking us how to fly!' John guessed, when they realised that they didn't have a Neverland dictionary. It certainly looked that way because the penguins started frantically flapping their wings. But their wings were so pathetically small – and their white tummies so fat from all the fish they had eaten – that it really was rather hopeless. Peter was quite unsympathetic towards them, saying it was their own faults for not going on a diet, but Wendy took pity on them and sprinkled their wings with a pouch of fairy dust. The penguins could now fly just like the graceful birds that they probably were long ago!

Remove one of the FAIRY DUST CARDS from your TOP-HAT CARD. Now go to 109.

249

Since Peter didn't have a dictionary, they couldn't understand a single word of Captain Hook's address. This incensed the pirate so much that he ordered his men to make the children walk the plank! Wendy was forced to go first but just before she reached the end, John tried to make a deal with the Captain. He removed a pouch of fairy dust from under his top-hat, offering it in return for their lives. There was a moment of anxiety while the Captain considered but at last he agreed and Wendy was, so to speak, let off the hook!

Remove one of the FAIRY DUST CARDS from your TOP-HAT CARD. Now go to 36.

250

'There's the waterfall!' Wendy exclaimed as she suddenly spotted it below. It was the most beautiful waterfall she had ever seen – full of torrents and rainbows. They had only flown a little way past it when Michael asked his sister how much further the sea was. His arms felt as if they were about to drop right off! 'I'm not sure, Michael,' Wendy replied, 'but I'll ask Peter to look up the waterfall on his map. That should give us an idea.'

Use your MAP to find which square the waterfall is in – then follow the appropriate instruction. If you don't have one, you'll have to guess which instruction to follow.

If you think D2	go to 240
If you think D1	go to 21
If you think D3	go to 261

251

'*Stop holding Peter's hand or I'll pull your hair!*' Wendy translated Tinker Bell's gabble as soon as Peter had given her his dictionary. Wendy went rather red as she handed the dictionary back. 'Why does she mind you holding my hand?' Peter asked bewilderedly. 'It was only because you were frightened of falling, wasn't it?' Wendy went an even deeper red and did not reply. But she decided perhaps it best *not* to hold his hand in future! ***Go to 196.***

252

Unhappily, Peter *hadn't* remembered to bring the magic spell book with him and so Michael just continued to fall. 'Quick, Peter, think of something else!' Wendy cried at him but Peter said he wasn't really in the mood for thinking. 'Perhaps I'll be more in the mood in an hour or two,' he told her simply. John, fortunately, had his wits about him. He whipped a pouch of fairy dust from under his hat and hurled it down at Michael. It hit him smack on the head, its contents bursting all over his curly hair. Poor Michael had a bit of a headache but at least he could fly again!

Remove one of the FAIRY DUST CARDS from your TOP-HAT CARD. Now go to 132.

253

Now they'd had a little rest after their long flight, Wendy said she thought it was about time she was introduced to the lost boys. 'Where are they?' she asked, looking all around. 'I thought they would have been here to welcome me!' Peter went a little red, explaining that they were on the other side of the island. 'I thought we'd have a few adventures first,' he told her coyly. 'That's why I decided to land *here* instead of near their home.' Anyway, to make Wendy happier, he said he would magic one of the lost boys over to them. All it took was the right magic spell word!

Use your MAGIC SPELL BOOK to find the right magic spell

word by placing exactly over the shape below – then follow the appropriate instruction. If you don't have one, you'll have to guess which instruction to follow.

If you think it's MERMAID	go to 80
If you think it's RAINBOW	go to 15
If you think it's DRAGON	go to 115

```
N  L D F    M     I E
  H  E R D    E B   A
    A   R    L K N
   K G H  G    M    E
   D R  N  A K E    D
   B B  F  I O N A  D
     N L   E K H    H
   H F B R D T O W W N
```

'*To Smugglers Caves!*' Wendy read out, using the dictionary to translate what the signpost said. No sooner had the word 'smugglers' been uttered, then Peter insisted that they go there. So too did John and Michael! 'Oh, all right then,' Wendy agreed, seeing that she was outnumbered, 'but if we meet any smugglers we're to have nothing to do with them. We shouldn't mix with their sort!' It wasn't long before they arrived at the little beach with the caves and much to Wendy's relief (and the boys' disappointment) there wasn't a smuggler in sight. They did find a magic spell book though – half-buried in the sand!

If you don't already have it there, put the MAGIC SPELL BOOK CARD into your CHARACTER CARD. Now go to 176.

255

John reached the redskin camp first, arriving right in the middle of a noisy dance. The redskins stamped their feet and made strange whooping sounds. 'Is it a war dance?' Wendy asked Peter anxiously but Peter shook his head. 'No, they're not in a war mood today,' he said, rather disappointedly. 'This is a rain dance to make it rain.' Wendy glanced up at the sky to see if the dance was having any effect but there wasn't a single cloud there – not even a tiny, fluffy one. So, she suggested that Peter help them by casting a magic spell to make it rain.

Use your MAGIC SPELL BOOK to find the right magic word

for this spell by placing exactly over the shape below – then follow the appropriate instruction. If you don't have one, you'll have to guess which instruction to follow.

If you think it's STORM   go to 146
If you think it's THUNDER   go to 283
If you think it's DOWNPOUR   go to 221

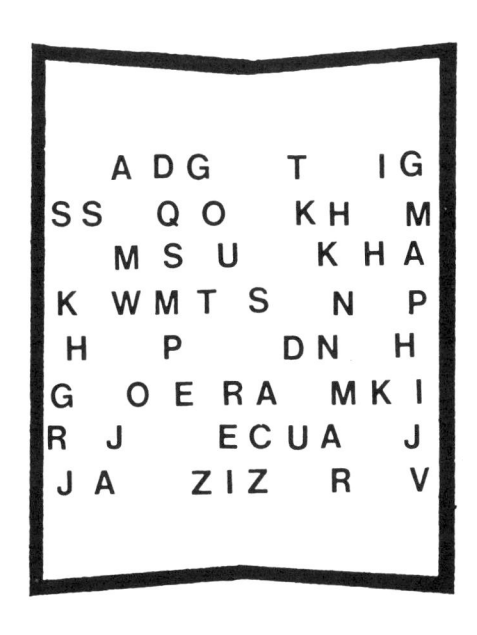

```
    A D G     T     I G
S S   Q O     K H     M
    M S U     K H   A
K   W M T S   N     P
H     P       D N   H
G   O E R A   M K I
R J       E C U A     J
J A     Z I Z   R     V
```

256

Much to Wendy's surprise, the wolf's howls were saying something friendly. 'It's asking if it can be my pet,' she translated with Peter's dictionary. 'It says it's never been anyone's pet before!' Well, Wendy was quite naturally touched by this but she did see certain practical problems. How was the wolf going to fly with them and was it house-trained? So she reluctantly left the wolf behind but she did give it the lost boys' address ('*The Hollowed-Out Trees, Neverland*') in case it ever wanted to call on them. ***Go to 38.***

257

Leaping off the cliff, the children flew down to join the mermaids' hand-bubble game in the water. The mermaids weren't quite as enchanting and friendly as they appeared, though. The only one they wanted on their team was Peter – Wendy, John and Michael had to make up the opposing team. The mermaids then tried every cheating tactic they knew to make sure they won. They pinched, shoved and pulled hair! At one point they even knocked off John's top-hat, causing one of the fairy dust pouches to fall out. It quickly sank to the seabed!

Remove one of the FAIRY DUST CARDS from your TOP-HAT CARD. Now go to 40.

258

Wendy suddenly glimpsed a beautiful silvery tail flash in the water! 'I think there's a mermaid just down there!' she said, pointing to her left. She was absolutely right because a few moments later, the mermaid pulled herself up on to a rock, and started to comb her hair. 'Oh, let's go down and make her acquaintance!' Wendy proposed ecstatically but the mermaid didn't seem quite as pleased to meet Wendy as Wendy was to meet her. With a bad-tempered look on her face, she suddenly started gabbling something at Wendy in Neverlander!

Use your NEVERLAND DICTIONARY to find out what the mermaid was saying by translating the instruction in her speech-balloon below. If you don't have one, go to 99 instead.

DIDDLY PUTT LIG UCK SUL WAP

259

Peter gnashed his teeth as he discovered that he had forgotten his telescope! He was just deciding that he would have to do without one when an anguished cry came echoing up the inside of the tree. 'Oh, Peter, I've just found this note from Captain Hook, the pirate,' a tearful Wendy told him when he had slid down to the underground house again. 'He says that he has taken the lost boys off to his ship as prisoners!' Peter was quick to respond, ordering that they fly off immediately in search of Hook's ship. Since there would be no time for stops on the flight, he instructed John to give them all a good sprinkling of fairy dust just in case.

Remove a FAIRY DUST CARD from your TOP-HAT CARD. Now go to 98.

260

'I think they're asking us if we would teach them to fly,' Wendy guessed when Peter confessed that he didn't have his dictionary. She said this because the Eskimoes kept flapping their arms. On the other hand, though, it might just have been a habit they'd developed because of the constantly cold weather! 'No, I think it's definitely that they want to be taught to fly,' John said as the Eskimoes now pointed up into the air. John therefore took out a pouch of fairy dust and sprinkled all the Eskimoes with it. He'd completely forgotten that they might later need it for themselves!

Remove one of the FAIRY DUST CARDS from your TOP-HAT CARD. Now go to 181.

261

Peter and the children at last arrived at the sea and it wasn't long after that they spotted Hook's ship! 'Follow me, lads!' Peter said, swooping down towards it. Wendy wanted to remind him that not all his company were lads but she thought it wrong to distract him just at the moment. As soon as they had alighted on the ship, Peter whipped out his sword, calling Hook's name. 'Your life is mine, Hook!' he cried as his arch-enemy appeared, and a furious duel commenced between them. As the children nervously watched, John sprinkled them all with a pouch of fairy dust. If Peter should lose the fight and Hook turned on them, he wanted to be sure they could make a swift getaway!

Remove a FAIRY DUST CARD from your TOP-HAT CARD. Now go to 11. (Remember: when there are no FAIRY DUST CARDS left in your TOP-HAT CARD the game is over, and you must start again from the beginning.)

262

'There are no more pirates than we can handle!' Peter said simply, looking through his telescope. He couldn't be bothered to try and count them! 'But how alert do they look – and are they *armed*?' Wendy asked cautiously. These were rather superfluous details for Peter, though, and he immediately led the flight down towards the ship. 'Hook – it's your life or mine!' he cried at his arch-enemy as he whipped out his sword. ***Go to 11.***

263

'The Never horse is asking if we would like a ride some of the way to Neverland,' Peter translated for them after he had produced his dictionary from under his belt. The others thought it would be a delightful idea. It would save some of their flying energy as well. So they all mounted the magical horse's back, holding on tight to its flowing, silvery mane. Just as the time came at last to take their leave of the horse, John noticed that it held a magic spell book in its mouth. 'It must be offering it to us as a present!' he exclaimed.

If you don't already have it there, put the MAGIC SPELL BOOK CARD into the slit of your CHARACTER CARD. Now go to 132.

264

They were just about to start the race when they heard a loud bang from below. Seconds later, a large round ball came whizzing past their ears! 'Oh, Peter, what is it?' Wendy asked anxiously, shaking all over. Peter seemed perfectly calm about it, though. 'Oh, it's just a cannonball,' he said breezily. 'I expect someone was trying to hit us.' This made Wendy shake even more and she asked Peter if he had a telescope with him so they could find out who this awful person was.

Use your TELESCOPE to see where the cannonball was coming from by placing exactly over the shape below – then follow the instruction. If you don't have one, go to 91 instead.

```
R  G S V O W Z   T W  B E O  E G
   S  O Q T   N   W  E N O M    J
S U F  E   I F B V  A  E   N    G
   Y T  S   H N I   R L X   E M E
```

265

'There's nothing in there but darkness!' Peter announced as he pointed his telescope into the cave. Wendy was very relieved at this but Peter only seemed disappointed. Anyway, he hoped there might be some beast or other lurking much further in and so he led the way into the cave's dark interior. The cave went on and on, promising horrors at every twist and turn, but the promises were never fulfilled and they at last emerged on to a sandy beach. 'I told you there was nothing in there!' Peter said, pretending to be cheerful about it. *Go to 176.*

266

'The chief is saying that yours is the nicest hair he has ever seen,' Peter translated for Wendy when he had arrived with his dictionary. 'He would like to take your scalp,' he added, 'so he can wear your hair on his belt!' Well, Wendy was naturally very flattered by this compliment about her hair but letting the chief take her scalp was quite out of the question. 'I perfectly agree,' said Peter, 'let's fight them!' The children fought very bravely but the redskins heavily outnumbered them and soon forced their surrender! *Go to 200.*

267

Peter now suggested making an attack on the redskins but Wendy was not very keen on the idea. She asked what the redskins would do if they captured them. 'Oh, scalp us probably,' Peter replied quite cheerfully. Wendy was a little comforted, though, by the discovery of a Neverland dictionary near the rock. This meant that she would now be able to speak to the redskin chief if they were captured – and she was sure she could win him over. Well, this was soon to be put to the test because the attack went very badly and the children were quickly overpowered!

If you don't already have it there, put the NEVERLAND DICTIONARY CARD into your CHARACTER CARD. Now go to 200.

268

John spotted the waterfall first – and, very soon after, he spotted the sea as well. They now started searching for Hook's ship but, as they were flying over the blue expanse of the sea, Wendy noticed something very peculiar below. The sea was swirling round and round, just like bathwater disappearing down the plug-hole! 'Oh, that's the Neverland whirlpool,' Peter told her, as if it should have been quite obvious! Wendy asked if she could look it up on his map so she would know exactly where they were.

Use your MAP to find which square the whirlpool is in – then follow the appropriate instruction. *If you don't have one, you'll have to guess which instruction to follow.*

If you think E1	go to 140
If you think E2	go to 230
If you think D1	go to 164

269

'It says that it saw Captain Hook's ship about three hundred flaps away,' Wendy informed the others as she used Peter's dictionary to translate the Never bird's reply. The children therefore counted out the three hundred flaps themselves and, sure enough, there was Hook's ship basking in the sun below! Peter immediately led the swoop down on it, drawing out his sword as they alighted on the ship's deck. 'Hook!' he cried. 'Prepare to meet thy doom!' ***Go to 11.***

270

'*FOXGLOVE!*' Peter shouted at the top of his voice when he had consulted his magic spell book. The spell worked instantly, and the cloud immediately disappeared! Peter was just about to return the book under his belt when he noticed a Neverland map tucked between two of the pages. 'Oh, clever me!' he cried, dancing up and down. 'I'm not quite so forgetful as I thought!'

If you don't already have it there, put the MAP into the CHARACTER CARD. Now go to 196.

271

'I don't have my magic spell book,' Peter told Wendy tearfully, 'so I don't know what the right word is to magic her better!' His little shoulders heaved as he sobbed. 'Don't worry, Peter,' Wendy said kindly, 'I'm sure we'll think of some other way to bring her back to life again.' They all thought as hard as they could and, suddenly, John had an idea. 'I know!' he said. 'We could try sprinkling one of the pouches of fairy dust over her.' The idea worked – for no sooner had the dust settled on Tinker Bell, than her light suddenly went on again. In no time at all, it was as bright as it had ever been!

Remove one of the FAIRY DUST CARDS from your TOP-HAT CARD. Now go to 123.

272

A little tinkle of her bell showed that Tinker Bell had spotted the ice-cream tree first. 'Well done, Tink!' Peter said as she led the way towards it. 'Since you were so clever, we'll let you gather the ice-cream for us!' So Tinker Bell flew up into the ice-cream tree's branches, pulling off the cornets. She brought down a chocolate one for Peter, a strawberry one for John and a vanilla one for Michael. 'Don't forget Wendy's,' Peter called up – and Tinker Bell suddenly hurled one down into Wendy's face! 'Just wait until I catch you, Tink!' Peter shouted up angrily but she had hidden herself somewhere behind the leaves. He quickly searched for his telescope so he could try and spot her.

Use your TELESCOPE to find Tinker Bell by placing exactly over the shape below – then follow the instruction. If you don't have one, go to 35 instead.

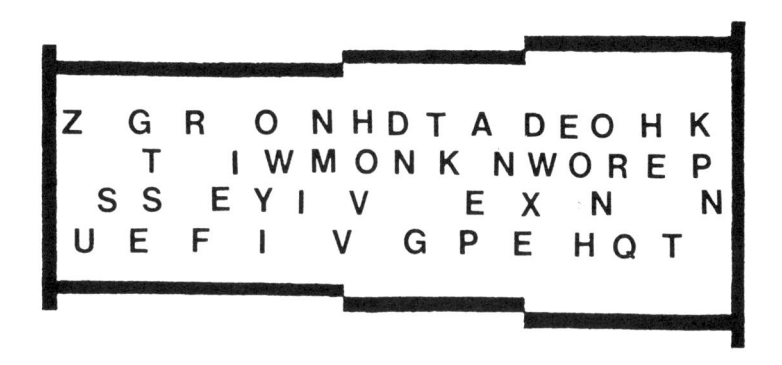

```
Z  G  R    O  N H D T  A    D E O  H   K
     T     I W M O N K    N W O R E P
  S  S    E Y I  V        E     X   N          N
U  E    F  I    V    G  P    E    H Q  T
```

273

Wendy's doubts were justified because Peter *didn't* have his magic spell book. 'Anyway, it was a good idea, Peter!' Wendy tried to console him as the pirates now roughly pushed them towards the dreaded plank. The pirates chose Michael to walk the plank first but, just as they were about to force him over the end with the tips of their swords, they changed their minds. The children were delighted, thinking they'd had a reprieve, but Peter was to disappoint them. 'They're just waiting until there are more sharks in the water!' he explained gravely. ***Go to 36.***

274

'I've spotted a mermaid, I've spotted one!' Peter cried joyously as he peered through his telescope. He defiantly poked his tongue out at Tinker Bell – a gesture which Wendy found a touch childish! They now all flew down to have a chat with the mermaid but they forgot that they couldn't speak her language. Fortunately, the mermaid had a Neverland dictionary with her, which she gave to the children to help them.

*If you don't already have it there, put the **NEVERLAND DICTIONARY CARD** into your **CHARACTER CARD**. Now go to 40.*

275

'I've forgotten my magic spell book,' Peter told Wendy, laughing rather heartlessly. 'You'll just have to have green hair for ever!' But his laughter soon died as he saw Wendy break down into tears. He didn't like to see Wendy crying. 'I know what we'll do,' he said, more sympathetically, 'we'll fly up into that sunray over there. That should turn your hair golden again!' Indeed, it did but it was such a long flight up to the sunray that John had to sprinkle them all with another pouch of fairy dust. But Wendy, for one, thought it was well and truly worth it!

*Remove one of the **FAIRY DUST CARDS** from your **TOP-HAT CARD**. Now go to 28.*

276

Although Peter didn't have a dictionary, it was quite easy for them all to guess the reason for Smee's grief. The poor little man had obviously been marooned. 'That devil, Hook!' Peter proclaimed. 'He's obviously left his bo'sun out here to perish for some little misdemeanour or other!' It was just as he was speaking this that he spotted Hook's ship in the distance, and he excitedly led the flight towards it. 'Hook!' he cried as they alighted on the *Jolly Roger*'s deck. 'Draw your sword because it's you or me this time!' The children and Smee (for John had sprinkled him with a pouch of fairy dust so he could fly with them) watched anxiously as the duel began . . .

Remove a FAIRY DUST CARD from your TOP-HAT CARD. Now go to 11. (Remember: when there are no FAIRY DUST CARDS left in your TOP-HAT CARD the game is over, and you must start again.)

277

'There they are!' Peter cried with delight as he spotted the fairy dust pouches through his telescope. 'Wasn't it clever of me to bring a telescope along?' he added cockily. 'It saved us from having to fly all the way down to spot them!' Wendy couldn't abide anyone showing off and therefore took great pleasure in informing him that they were going to have to fly all the way down anyway. For, now they had spotted them, they had also to pick them up! ***Go to 132.***

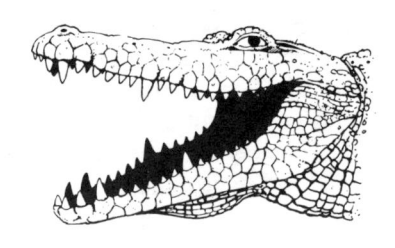

278

'I must have left the telescope in your bedroom,' Peter told Wendy when he had checked under his belt and found that it wasn't there. He didn't sound at all remorseful about it. In fact, he wasn't because, if it *was* Wendy's parents down there, he would rather she didn't know about it. It might make her change her mind and fly back again! To encourage them all to continue, he took a pinch of fairy dust from under John's hat and gave them a good sprinkling. It meant that they could now fly twice as fast!

Remove one of the FAIRY DUST CARDS from your TOP-HAT CARD. Now go to 196.

279

Suddenly, Wendy spotted a beautiful island – all shimmer and colour – way below. 'Oh, I'm sorry for doubting you, Peter,' she apologised. 'You didn't make a wrong turn after all. Look, there's Neverland – down there!' They all prepared to make their descent but Peter said it would be a lot easier if they just slid down the nearest rainbow. 'You see, all rainbows end in Neverland!' he told them. Unfortunately, though, there wasn't a rainbow in sight. 'Perhaps you could make one appear by saying one of your magic spell words, Peter,' Wendy suggested. 'Do you have your book with you to find out what the right word is?'

Use your MAGIC SPELL BOOK to find the right magic spell

***word by placing exactly over the shape below – then follow the
instruction. If you don't have one, you'll have to guess which
instruction to follow.***

If you think it's PURPLE	go to 174
If you think it's VIOLET	go to 122
If you think it's ORANGE	go to 92

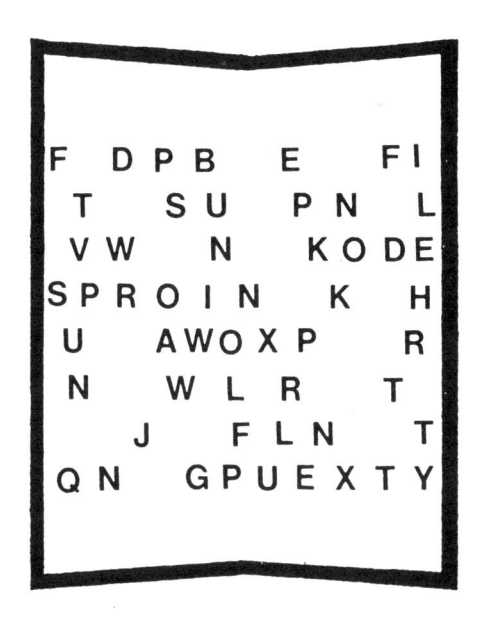

```
F   D P B    E      F I
 T    S U    P N     L
 V W    N      K O D E
S P R O I N    K     H
U    A W O X P       R
N    W  L R          T
    J    F L N       T
Q N     G P U E X T Y
```

280

'I'm sorry but I don't have my dictionary,' Peter told Wendy after checking under his belt. He wasn't that sorry, though, because he thought it better if Wendy was kept ignorant of what Tinker Bell was saying! Wendy then asked Peter to translate for her himself but Peter said he couldn't without his dictionary. That may have been true or it may not! John soon drew their attention to more important matters, however. For, he had burst one of his pouches of fairy dust when he had bumped to the ground. He quickly asked everyone to help him gather up the contents – but a gust of wind suddenly came along and scattered the dust out to sea!

Remove one of your FAIRY DUST CARDS from your TOP-HAT CARD. Now go to 103.

281

'Can't you try and remember at least a *bit* of Neverlander?' Wendy implored Peter when he told her that he didn't have his dictionary. 'Then we wouldn't need a dictionary anyway!' Peter tried as hard as he could, knitting his brows and gritting his little teeth, but it just wouldn't work. 'I'm sorry, Wendy,' he said, 'but, you see, it was all of three days ago that I was last in Neverland . . . and that's an awfully long time to try and remember things!' So they decided just to forget about the signpost and flew up into the air to see where the breezes carried them. They at last came to land on a little sandy beach. 'After all that flying,' said the exhausted John, 'I think we'd better have another sprinkle of fairy dust!'

Remove one of the FAIRY DUST CARDS from your TOP-HAT CARD. Now go to 176.

282

Tinker Bell reached the redskin camp first, coming to land on a large crag that overlooked it. As soon as the others had landed, they kept their heads down in case they were seen. 'Let's make a surprise attack on them,' Peter whispered eagerly but Wendy strictly forbade it. When Peter went into a sulk, however, she agreed to compromise. "All right, we'll make an attack as long as there aren't more than a dozen redskins,' she offered. She suggested Peter use his telescope to make the counting easier.

Use your TELESCOPE to obtain a better view of the redskins by placing exactly over the shape below – then follow the instruction. If you don't have one, go to 67 instead.

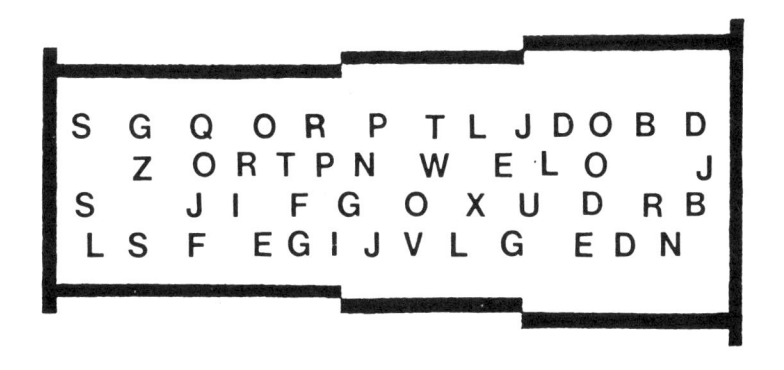

```
S  G  Q  O  R  P  T L J D O B  D
   Z  O R T P N  W  E L O      J
S     J I  F  G  O X U  D  R B
L  S  F  E G I J V  L  G   E D N
```

283

Peter said he didn't have his magic spell book, though – and, even if he did, he didn't want to make it rain! 'Everything just gets wet and drippy!' he said. Wendy tried to explain that it was sometimes good for things to become wet and drippy – it helped them to grow. But mention of the word 'grow' only made Peter a whole lot worse. It was the most unlikeable word he knew! ***Go to 125.***

284

'Not to worry,' said Peter breezily when he told the others that he didn't have his magic spell book, 'we can have a make-believe breakfast!' Peter seemed to enjoy the make-believe breakfast as much as a real one, heartily tucking in to his imaginary plateful, but Wendy, Michael and John weren't quite so enthusiastic about it. It didn't seem to fill that terrible hole in their tummies! And nor did it give them as much energy as a real breakfast for, when they were ready to fly away from the cave, they found that they could barely leave the ground. John had to sprinkle them with another pouch of fairy dust to remedy the situation.

Remove one of the FAIRY DUST CARDS from your TOP-HAT CARD. Now go to 38.